Equity Compensation for Limited Liability Companies

Companies

SECOND EDITION

Equity Compensation for Limited Liability Companies

SECOND EDITION

Teresa Y. Huang • David R. Johanson • Samuel W. Krause
Rachel J. Markun • Alan Nadel • Monica R. Patel • Corey Rosen

The National Center for Employee Ownership
Oakland, California

This publication is designed to provide accurate and authoritative information in regard to the subject matter covered. It is sold with the understanding that the publisher is not engaged in rendering legal, accounting, or other professional service. If legal advice or other expert assistance is required, the services of a competent professional person should be sought.

Legal, accounting, and other rules affecting business often change. Before making decisions based on the information you find here or in any publication from any publisher, you should ascertain what changes might have occurred and what changes might be forthcoming. The NCEO's Web site (including the members-only area) and newsletter for members provide regular updates on these changes. If you have any questions or concerns about a particular issue, check with your professional advisor or, if you are an NCEO member, call or email us.

Equity Compensation for Limited Liability Companies, 2nd Ed.
Teresa Y. Huang, David R. Johanson, Samuel W. Krause, Rachel J. Markun, Alan Nadel, Monica R. Patel, and Corey Rosen

Book design by Scott S. Rodrick

The National Center for Employee Ownership
1736 Franklin Street, 8th Floor
Oakland, CA 94612
(510) 208-1300
(510) 272-9510 (fax)
Web site: www.nceo.org

ISBN: 978-1-938220-07-4

Contents

Sample plan documents included on the print book's CD and in the digital book's zipped file (see the descriptions in the appendix):
Equity Incentive Plan
Capital Interests or Profits Interests Award Agreement
Summary Memorandum
Action by Unanimous Written Consent of the Voting Members
Units Appreciation Rights Plan
Units Appreciation Rights Agreement
Action by Unanimous Written Consent of the Voting Members (units plan)
David R. Johanson, Rachel J. Markun, Teresa Y. Huang, and Monica R. Patel

Preface

Corey Rosen

Founder, National Center for Employee Ownership (NCEO)

For many years, the most common advice on sharing equity with employees in a limited liability company (LLC) has been "switch to S corporation status instead." The argument was that it was too complicated to share equity in an LLC. Yet many LLC company leaders want to share equity with employees and have very good reasons for retaining their company's status as an LLC. When I asked experts in employee ownership law if it were possible to share equity in an LLC, the usual response was "yes, but it is complicated." No one seemed to want to go into too much detail about just what these complications were, however.

So after many years of telling people that, yes, it is possible, but that we did not have any specific material or advice on the topic (because we could not find anyone who had written about it in more than the most general terms), we decided to create our own material. This book is the product of that effort. It is, we believe, the only detailed exploration of equity compensation in limited liability companies available.

The book starts with a general description of LLCs and an overview of the ways to share equity. Chapter 2 explores alternative approaches to designing plans in terms of who gets what, how much they get, when they get it, and what triggers the awards. Chapter 3 provides a detailed look at the various specific ways to share equity in an LLC, including capital interests, profits interests, unit plans, and unit appreciation plans. The chapter also addresses tax and regulatory issues. Chapter 4 describes how these plans affect a company's financial statements. Chapter 5 discusses the various kinds of equity-sharing methods available in S or C corporations. The idea here is to let readers judge whether the somewhat broader range of choices for such corporations justifies switching from LLC status. Finally, chapter 6 explains various approaches to communicating equity compensation plans.

The comprehensive set of plan documents included in electronic form provides plan language, grant agreements, and board approval agreements for the various kinds of awards. These model plans are not "cut and paste." Instead, they are intended to help readers think through the various issues and requirements for plans so that when they do go to a qualified attorney, they can make sure their plans have the elements they need.

About the Second Edition

The book was substantially revised and expanded for the second edition. The main chapter, on equity interests in LLCs (chapter 3) was completely rewritten and expanded by a team of experienced attorneys. The same team replaced the single plan document in the first edition of the book with a new, complete set of plan documents. (These are not printed as part of the text but rather provided electronically as Word documents; see the appendix for details.) Additionally, chapter 6 has been added, discussing communicating with employees about equity. Finally, the chapter on accounting has been updated.

Chapter 1

A Primer on Limited Liability Companies

Corey Rosen

Limited liability companies (LLCs) have become a very popular way to organize new and smaller enterprises. They offer the advantages of partnership taxation treatment (although a choice can be made to be taxed as a corporation), limited personal liability for the owners, flexibility in the distribution of earnings, flatter governance and management structure, and fewer paperwork requirements than S or C corporations. On the other hand, they do require that owners pay income taxes on their share of company earnings even if not distributed, often are not attractive to venture capital and private equity investors, and face differing laws in various states. Furthermore, the LLC structure is more cumbersome and a less efficient vehicle for offering equity compensation to employees than S or C corporations are.

LLC owners often say that they formed their company as an LLC because their attorney or advisor said they should. While some people clearly think through the pros and cons of different legal forms for conducting their business, others just take this advice without questioning whether an LLC really is the best choice. This book provides a basic overview of LLC issues. Because state laws for LLCs vary, and tax and other requirements can vary even more, it is important for business owners to work closely with their advisors to make sure they understand all the implications of choosing the LLC form of business. No one publication can provide the kind of detailed advice applicable to every situation.

What Is an LLC?

The limited liability company is a relatively new type of business form. Wyoming passed the first LLC law in 1977; the other states eventually followed suit. While the laws for LLCs are similar from one jurisdiction to another and sometimes identical, they are not all the same. Some states impose entity taxes on LLCs; a few impose some level of income tax. A few states have different governance requirements as well. If an LLC operates in more than one state, it may be subject to multiple tax and possibly governance rules.

The impetus behind the creation of LLC law was to provide a more simple and flexible way for small businesses to organize than corporate law usually permits. It was intended that businesses would be taxed as proprietorships or partnerships while providing their owners with the limited liability available to corporate shareholders. LLCs are owned by "members" rather than shareholders. The term is roughly analogous to partners or shareholders, but with some notable differences. LLCs must have at least two members if they are to be taxed as partnerships (a one-owner LLC will be taxed as a sole proprietorship or a corporation for federal tax purposes). The members create an "operating agreement" that functions similarly to a corporation's bylaws. The agreement specifies how the LLC will be governed and managed, how profits and losses will be allocated, and what the member rights are (including voting, buy-sell arrangements, and distributions of earnings). LLC agreements can specify whether a member will be the manager or someone else will serve in that capacity.

Key Organizational Issues

Limited Liability

Like corporate shareholders, LLC members can avoid personal responsibility for losses or liabilities of the LLC beyond what the LLC can pay. This is not an unlimited right, however. Several circumstances can still "pierce the corporate veil" and give rise to personal liability, including:

- Contracts that members sign, such as personal guarantees for debt or performance

- Failure to deposit taxes withheld from employee wages
- Intentional fraud, reckless behavior, or illegal acts
- Personal and direct injury of someone or property

In some cases, the "corporate veil" may also be pierced if tax authorities can sustain the position that the LLC is really not an entity separate from a member's personal interests. Establishing one's house as an LLC to avoid personal liability for defaulting on the underlying mortgage, for instance, would not be effective protection.

Governance

Unlike a corporation, an LLC does not require a board of directors, although some kind of governing or advisory body may be advisable and may be required if there are outside investors. Instead, an LLC's members make decisions about the company subject to the operating agreement. A few states require more formal governance procedures, however, such as an annual member meeting, something normally only required of a corporation.

Allocation of Earnings

Unlike S or C corporations, LLCs need not allocate earnings pro rata to capital ownership. In an S corporation, owners receive a share of earnings based on their respective percentages of corporate ownership; in C corporations, distributions of earnings are based on specified stock rights but must be proportional to ownership within the same classes of stock. LLC members are taxed not necessarily based on their membership interest percentage, but rather based on whatever agreement the members have made for allocating earnings. This agreement may be stated in the operating agreement, may take the form of income-only partnership interests, or may be just an understanding among the LLC members.

Another difference between a corporation and an LLC is the manner and extent to which the business's earnings are allocated annually. In the case of an LLC, all of the net income of the business is allocable to the members who pay personal income tax on their respective amounts regardless of distributions they receive during the applicable year. Similarly to partners in a partnership, the LLC members may agree that a partner may be allocated a disproportionate percentage of the LLC earnings based on whatever business factors they choose.

This flexibility is one of the major advantages of an LLC. It is especially useful in the case of LLCs where one party invests capital (e.g., venture capital or private equity) and another puts in "sweat equity" (i.e., performance of services for less than full pay). In an S corporation, for instance, if a shareholder purchases 20% of the corporate stock, then he or she will be allocated 20% of the corporate net earnings. But if that same 20% shareholder purchases 20% of the stock and also puts in a year of sweat equity to build the business, he or she may not receive more than a 20% share of the corporate net income, although the parties could agree to also pay additional compensation in recognition of the shareholder's efforts. In the same situation with an LLC, however, the LLC members may simply choose to allocate a greater portion of the company's net earnings to that individual to compensate for sweat equity. Alternatively, they may agree to compensate the individual by awarding more ownership (i.e., member units) in the LLC.

The allocation-of-earnings approach must have a substantial economic effect; i.e., there must be a good business reason for doing it, other than to avoid taxation. Provided the allocation of earnings is not based on tax avoidance, the allocation generally will be respected by the IRS. Allocating more earnings to an owner with a lower tax rate and less to one with a higher rate, absent some other compelling business reason, likely would be problematic. Similarly, care should be taken with the allocation of passive income and losses in an LLC, a subject beyond the scope of this primer. This should be discussed with a tax professional prior to making any special allocations of income or loss.

Members

S corporations are permitted to have up to 100 shareholders and still retain the S corporation status. In contrast, LLCs and C corporations may have an unlimited number of members or shareholders. S corporations may have only one class of stock; LLCs and C corporations can have different rights attributed to different classes of ownership. S corporations may not be owned by certain prohibited entities, including C corporations, other S corporations, most non-taxable entities, most trusts, other LLCs, partnerships, or nonresident aliens. LLCs may be owned by anyone. LLCs are rarely used in some industries (e.g., venture capital) because the associated tax effects are inconsistent with the objectives of the owners. LLC members also may have different rights or benefits attached to their ownership besides how earnings are allocated, such as special distributions, governance, or the ability to cash out their ownership interests.

Dissolution

The LLC has a permanent life unless a time of dissolution is specified in the operating agreement. Similarly, one or more members may leave and the other members agree to continue the business. The operating agreement must be specific on this eventuality to avoid inadvertent termination.

Mergers and Other Ownership Transfers

If an LLC is merged into another company, it is not eligible for tax-free reorganization as provided by Internal Revenue Code Section 368. The LLC can first be terminated and S or C status chosen, but if the change and merger come within a close time frame, it will likely be considered a "step transaction," whereby the IRS takes the position that it is still an LLC.

LLCs can, however, be sold to other companies just like corporations, subject to the tax issues discussed below. Ownership interests can also be transferred to anyone or any entity, with some restrictions varying by state. In S corporations, by contrast, transfers can be made only to other S owners.

Taxes

A limited liability company is taxed as a sole proprietorship (if there is only one owner) or a partnership unless the LLC "checks the box" on an IRS filing to be taxed as a corporation. As a sole proprietorship or partnership, members are taxed on their pro-rata share of earnings unless the operating agreement specifies otherwise. This is the share of the actual earnings of the LLC, not the earnings that are distributed (earnings may be retained to grow the company, for instance). These earnings, in turn, are taxed at the individual member's personal tax rates. Members usually must make quarterly estimated income tax payments. While the federal government levies no tax on the LLC, some states do.

One difference between an LLC and an S corporation or C corporation is the manner in which earnings are subject to payroll taxes. In a corporation, when a shareholder-employee receives compensation, the employee pays half of the payroll taxes (through withholding) and the company pays the other half. In an LLC, the member pays the full amount of the payroll taxes in the form of self-employment tax. The total is currently 12.4% of pay up to the current year's Social Security wage base for the Social Security component of self-employment tax, plus 2.9% of all pay for the Medicare component. Although the LLC member pays twice what an S corporation shareholder pays, they both pay the same when the S corporation's share of taxes is also considered.

Another difference between a corporation and an LLC is the manner and extent to which the business's earnings are taxed each year. In the case of an LLC, all of the net income of the business is allocable to the members who pay personal income tax on their allocated amounts regardless of distributions they receive during the applicable year. If a member has a 40% interest in an LLC and the LLC earns a profit of $100,000 during the year, that member is allocated $40,000 of income even if he or she receives only a $20,000 distribution. On the other hand, a C corporation that earns a profit of $100,000 must pay corporate income tax on the full amount. If a distribution of that income (e.g., a dividend) is made to shareholders, they must pay income tax on those distributed amounts. Hence, the use of a C corporation usually results in double taxation of the corporate profits.

At the time of sale of LLC member units, a single capital gains tax generally is imposed on the gain (with some exceptions, e.g., receivables). This is different from a C (but not S) corporation, where an *asset* sale would trigger double taxation by virtue of a corporate capital gains tax on the appreciated value of the assets for the corporation and another capital gains tax for the shareholders on the sale of the company's shares.

A *stock* sale, however, generally is not subject to double taxation, and a merger for stock in the acquirer may be tax-deferred altogether.

Conclusion

The flexibility of LLCs makes them attractive vehicles for those who wish for the flexibility of a proprietorship or partnership while retaining legal protection for the owners. Unfortunately, while they are simpler and more flexible than C or S corporations, they are considerably less so on issues concerning equity compensation for employees. In fact, some advisors suggest that companies wishing to share equity with employees should select regular corporate status because employees more readily understand stock options and restricted stock than partnership interests. We believe they may be too hasty in their recommendations, as the rest of this book will show. Equity compensation in the case of an LLC can provide for significant incentives that are performance-based. The range of choices may be narrower in the case of an LLC, and there are some remaining tax uncertainties and complexities, but effective performance-based incentives certainly can be structured in the LLC.

Chapter 2

Designing an Equity Incentive Plan

Corey Rosen

A variety of issues must be considered when designing an equity compensation plan for employees in an LLC. This chapter is not intended to provide specific guidelines on how to structure a plan but rather to raise the issues companies need to consider. In making these decisions, company leaders should consult with peers and advisors as well as evaluate available survey data on industry practices.

How Much to Share

The first decision is how much ownership to share. The most typical way owners of closely held companies decide how much ownership to share is by setting aside an amount of equity or equity rights that is within the maximum dilution level with which they are comfortable. This approach can create problems, however.

Typically, once this number is set, a large portion of this equity is either provided immediately to existing employees or allocated to employees over a few years. The problem with this strategy is that allocating too much too quickly leaves relatively little equity to give to new employees. In a growing company, that can lead to a severe problem in attracting and retaining good people. It can also create two classes of employees, some with large equity grants and some without them. Moreover, this model often does not create an explicit link between employee effort and the rewards of ownership.

A second approach focuses on what percentage of compensation must be provided in the form of equity in order to attract, retain, and motivate people. These decisions need to be based on competitive considerations of what people could receive elsewhere as well as on discussions with employees to get a sense of how much they expect. Finding relevant information about competitive pay practices means more than simply referring to a salary survey. Competitive pay information should be based on data from companies that might compete for the same employees, rather than just the company's business competitors. Often this includes companies in other industries that may hire individuals with similar experiences and skill sets as those of the company's current employees.

Rather than thinking about "how much" in terms of a total percentage of company shares or total compensation, it might make sense to use a more dynamic model based on performance. In this approach, the issue for existing owners is not "what percentage of the company do we own?" but "how much is what we own worth?" Owners in this model would rather own 10% of an $11 million company than 90% of a $1 million company. This notion can be incorporated into an explicit plan by telling employees that if the company meets or exceeds certain targets, they will receive a percentage of the incremental value created by that performance in the form of equity or equity rights. If the company exceeds its goals, then, by definition, sharing part of the surplus value leaves both the employees and the existing owners better off than they would have been. The targets can be based on whatever performance goals are appropriate for the company, such as sales, profits, market penetration, or whatever else is critical to the company's future. Given the volatility in the economy over the last 15 years or so, the company should also include risk management considerations in the selection of relevant performance targets. Providing substantial equity grants when the company has an exceptionally good year or two may come back to haunt the company if the company's fortunes then decline for some period of time. Risk can be managed by putting caps on the total awards available under any target plan, for instance.

It is also important to consider the "internal equity" of awards. A common problem in equity plans is that employees believe they are not getting what they deserve, something they assess primarily based on what they perceive other people are receiving. Few employees would argue that everyone should be paid the same, but most would contend that everyone should receive awards consistent with their relative contributions to the company. This problem has been starkest in relationship to executive pay, but even at rank-and-file levels, it is not uncommon for companies to pay people doing very similar jobs very different amounts of equity, perhaps because of the timing of when they came to work (more awards were available or the shares were more opportunely priced) or what was perceived as necessary to hire them. Nobel Prize-winning research has shown that perceived equity in economic transactions will often trump purely "rational" economic logic. Employees will be more cynical and demotivated if they believe that their awards are inequitable relative to what top executives receive. Boards and compensation consultants may (rightly or wrongly) argue that this can benefit the entire company, but employees will be slower to accept these arguments than the CEO's peers. Fairness consistently shows up as one of the most, if not the most, important determinant of work motivation and turnover intention, so this is not a small issue.

The fairness issue often comes up in merit-based plans. While it might seem more fair and more efficient to give the lion's share of the awards to the best performers, research shows that about 70% of the work force believes it is in the top 10% of performers. Thus any merit-based program that loans awards to a relatively small group will create a lot of people who believe they are being treated unfairly. One way to help preserve the benefits of a merit-based approach and create more of a perception of fairness is get employee input into what the merit criteria should be. Even if the result is a somewhat broader or perhaps less economically "optimal" result, if employees buy into the formula in advance, then the unfairness problem can be significantly eased.

What Kind of Equity?

The kinds of equity vehicles a company chooses depend largely on the purposes of the plan. While that may seem obvious, it is far too common for companies to select an equity vehicle because "that's what other people do," or "that's what my advisor understood best," or "I didn't know there were other ways to do it." Beware of advisors whose discouragement of one kind of a plan or another may really be their way of saying, "I don't know how to do the other types."

Sharing equity in LLCs is more challenging than in S or C corporations. In fact, as noted in the preface to this book, advisors frequently tell clients that if they want to share equity with employees, they should switch to S corporation status, which allows them to use options, phantom stock, restricted stock, stock appreciation rights, and similar plans. S corporations are taxed similarly to LLCs, but are less flexible in terms of how earnings are distributed. While employee equity awards in LLCs present more complex tax considerations than is the case in S or C corporations, there are approaches that can be effective.

Forms of Equity Available in an LLC

There are two main forms of actual equity interests available in an LLC:[1]

- *Capital interests:* Capital interests can be compared to restricted stock in an S or C corporation. They grant the employee the right to share in the capital value of the company through the receipt of a share of the proceeds upon sale of the company.

- *Profits interests:* A profits interest will entitle the owner both to capital appreciation and profits of the business.

Either type of interest may be subject to restrictions, such as a vesting requirement. Either may be forfeited if the employee is engaged in wrongdoing at the company or goes to work for a competitor.

Options and Equity-Equivalent Rights

Rather than directly granting the above interests, companies can grant a right to acquire them later or the right to receive the equivalent of their value:

- *Options:* Companies can issue an option to acquire these interests at a later point based on a current price.

---

1. There is also the "carried interest" (particularly common in private equity and hedge funds structured as LLCs), which is not a form of equity but a right to share in the LLC's profits. It is little used in the equity compensation context addressed here and thus will not be discussed further.

- *Equity-equivalent rights (phantom equity):* Alternatively, the company can use equity-equivalent rights (also called "synthetic equity," "virtual options," "unit appreciation rights," and other names that help explain the concept), which are equivalent to stock appreciation rights in an S or C corporation. The company gives the employees a grant of a hypothetical number of capital interest or profit interest units. On vesting, any increase in the value of these units is paid in cash, much as a bonus would be paid. The right could also be structured so that the employee received the entire value of a capital or profits interest, somewhat like the grant of phantom shares in an S or C corporation. In this discussion, we will call awards that grant an increase in value "equity appreciation rights" and ones that provide the full value "phantom equity" (terminology parallel to the concepts of stock appreciation rights and phantom stock in C and S corporations).

Basic Tax Issues

An employee's receipt of a profits interest in exchange for services is not taxable upon grant if certain safe harbor tax requirements are satisfied, including the requirement that the interest not be sold within two years of receipt. If these requirements are not satisfied, there is some uncertainty about the income tax consequences arising from the grant of a profits interest to an employee. When the employee redeems his or her profits interest (by selling it back to the company or to a third party), the gain is taxed as either a short-term or long-term capital gain, depending upon how long the interest was held by the employee. It should be noted that some tax advisors have expressed concern about whether capital gain treatment is available for employees who initially received a profits interest for no cost, while other advisors do not share that concern. Employees with profits interests are taxed as partners rather than as employees, so their income is reported on a Schedule K-1 and is not subject to income tax withholding.

An employee who receives a capital interest in exchange for services recognizes compensation income in the year of the award. The amount of income that is recognized equals the fair market value of the interest at the time of grant, less anything paid by the employee for the capital interest. If the interest is subject to a substantial risk of forfeiture and is nontransferable, as is typically the case, then the recognition of ordinary income tax is delayed until the forfeiture restriction lapses, unless the employee makes a timely Section 83(b) election. If a Section 83(b) election is not made, then ordinary income tax is paid on the value of the award at the time it vests. Any additional appreciation in the value of the capital interest is subject to either long- or short-term capital gains tax, depending upon how long the capital interest is held following recognition of ordinary income. An employee can also make an 83(b) election on a profits interest, in which case the employee would be eligible for capital gains tax treatment on the sale of the resulting membership interest after exercise. If granted at fair market value, the initial grant has no current liquidation value (it has a value only if the unit price increases), so there would be no immediate tax obligation. In both cases, however, if an 83(b) election is made, the employee receives a K-1 statement requiring payment on a share of the LLC's earnings.

If a Section 83(b) election is made but the award never vests, the employee may not claim a refund from the IRS for the ordinary income taxes that were paid. The company receives a tax deduction for any amounts on which the employee pays ordinary income tax. Under the partnership taxation rules, there is a question about whether there is also a "deemed sale" when a capital interest is awarded or forfeited, resulting in potential income tax consequences for other holders of capital interests in the company.

Granting an option to acquire either a capital interest or profits interest is not a taxable event for either the employee or the company. The exercise of an option on a capital interest will result in taxable income for the employee and a deduction for the company. The exercise of an option on a profits interest would not be taxable for the employee or deductible for the company if the tax requirements for nonrecognition of tax on a profits interest were satisfied.

For tax purposes, equity appreciation rights are treated in the same way as a bonus: the employee pays ordinary income tax on the receipt of the cash award, and the company is entitled to a corresponding tax deduction.

Complexity Concerns

Many companies will choose one kind of award or another because it is less complex to administer, understand, and tax. This is more of an issue in an LLC, where the tax issues can be very complex and somewhat uncertain. In fact, this is why many advisors urge companies to switch to S status, where the tax issues are simpler. If employees find they have a great deal of difficulty understanding how an award works, or see the tax treatment as just too difficult to grasp relative to other kinds of pay, the value of the award can be diminished substantially. It might be better to choose a simpler alternative equity approach, such as equity-equivalent awards, even if these awards may have less favorable long-term tax consequences because they never qualify for capital gains treatment.

As with all the choices below, keep in mind that companies can give different employees different kinds or mixes of awards, with different rules being applicable to each.

Granting Existing Value or the Value of Future Increases Only

Capital interests, profits interests, or phantom equity give the employee the existing value of the ownership plus any appreciation (much like giving an employee a share with or without dividend rights in a corporation). That means the employee reaps the benefit of the embedded value that has been previously created. This would be most logical in cases where the company has been running for a while, and the early employees have not yet received any equity awards. "Full-value" awards effectively give these employees some retroactive benefit for their work. These awards also make sense if the intention is to ensure that employees receive something even if the value of the company does not increase or increases too slowly to make the awards appealing.

In contrast, options on a capital interest or profits interest, like equity appreciation rights, provide only a share in the future growth in value. If a company is granting awards very early on when there is little existing value, these appreciation-based awards can provide significant value to employees, much like full-value awards. Down the road, however, they are very different.

One problem with appreciation-based awards is that the single most important factor in determining their value is volatility. In the formula that accountants use to assess the present value of the award of a stock option, for instance, volatility is the single most important factor. This may seem counterintuitive. Wouldn't you prefer an option on a stock that has less dramatic ups and downs? But consider that with an option, you can ignore the downs (just don't exercise the options) and take advantage of the ups. A more stable stock has lower high points (but also higher low points), providing less of this leveraging opportunity.

This has a number of additional insidious effects. First, it can encourage excessive risk-taking by top decision-makers, especially if their expected time horizon with the company is shorter than the term of the equity award. Second, it introduces a lottery effect into the incentive structure. Two employees receiving identical awards may have significantly different opportunities for gains if they were hired at different dates when the equity had a different value. Finally, appreciation-based awards can engender cynicism among employees who view equity as a lottery whose benefits may go to the lucky and to the insiders who know best when to exercise.

This may be less of an issue in an LLC than it is in other companies, especially public companies. LLC valuations tend to be done annually, absent some specific event, and may "smooth out" some of the external factors that create volatility for stocks in general. Nonetheless, LLCs can still be subject to the same problems as corporations, especially if the market for their products or services is highly variable.

Who Is Eligible and Who Will Actually Get Equity?

In the past, the answer to the question of who was eligible was very simple for most companies: just the "key" people. In some ways, this is still how companies view equity; it is just that their definition of "key" has changed. For many companies, everyone is a key person. Many LLC companies have a flat management structure and are pushing down more decision-making to all levels, asking employees to make business decisions on a regular basis. Managers at these companies reason that if they want people to think and act like owners, they should make them owners. At the same time, for some companies in some labor markets, it is necessary to provide options at all levels just to attract and retain people. For companies in these situations, the answer to "who's eligible?" is simple—everyone is.

One set of issues that some companies consider, but that they probably should not, is the so-called "1/n" or "free rider" effect, and the related "line-of-sight" problem. The argument here is that an equity award cannot be much of an incentive to an employee who cannot see (has no line of sight to) just how his or her work actually affects the value of the business. This is especially problematic in larger organizations where employees not only don't have a clear line of sight to the award but also can figure they can "free ride" on the efforts of others.

These arguments are appealing but empirically wrong. Research shows that motivation at work is much more complicated than a simple economic calculation. Few employees go to work each day thinking, "If I do x, I get y, but if I do x + a, I get y + b, so if y + b is large enough, I'll do x + a." In reality, this is really not the case. Research shows again and again that most people's efforts at work are a function of how well their job functions fit their skills, whether they have opportunities for meaningful input into decisions affecting their jobs, how much they trust management and management trusts them, whether they find the job engaging, and whether they believe what they and the company do has value.

Equity sharing becomes important in this context not so much as an incentive for behavior but as a reward. If people are asked to act like owners and are treated like owners, they will be more productive and make larger contributions in terms of new ideas and information. If they then are denied an opportunity to benefit from what they add, they will feel manipulated and back away. If, on the other hand, they feel they are equitably rewarded relative to what others contribute or that they are all part of a team sharing in the results, they are much more likely to stay committed. So the question of who gets equity should be based on which employees should be thinking and acting like owners.

Tenure

At the simplest level, companies can require that people work a minimum amount of time, often one year, before they become eligible for equity awards. This ensures that each employee has at least some commitment to the company.

Full-Time/Part-Time

In the past, it was unusual to provide equity to part-time employees. Innovators like Southwest Airlines, however, have provided options to everyone, arguing that many of their part-time people would (or if properly rewarded could) become long-term employees.

Performance or a Universal Rule?

Equity can be granted according to some kind of merit judgment; on a regular, universal schedule such as annually, or upon hiring or promotion; or it can be granted or vest upon the achievement of individual, group, or corporate objectives. These methods are not mutually exclusive; many companies use a combination of these techniques.

The core issue here is that, on the one hand, including everyone who is eligible according to some formula rules out management discretion, which employees may see as arbitrary or political. It also may help foster a team atmosphere in which everyone sees that they have a stake. On the other hand, some employees may feel cheated if they think they have been exceptional performers but receive unexceptional rewards. This suggests that some combination of the two can be appealing, provided the basis for rewarding excellence is one that most or all employees see as reasonably fair—a tricky business, but one many companies have done well at, albeit in a variety of ways. Some companies, for instance, use 360-degree performance reviews in which everyone reviews everyone else, others use very specific and transparent financial or other measurable targets, and others seek employee input in designing rating systems.

A typical merit-based approach would provide work unit managers (or a single manager in a smaller company) with a number of awards that can be granted to employees in the group based on performance appraisals. An alternative to individual merit judgments is to provide that a pool of equity awards will be given to a work team upon the achievement of the team's goals. Many companies, of course, will simply name specific individuals, usually top managers, who will receive equity, but the company will define their allocation based on merit assessments of some sort.

At the other end of the spectrum is an automatic formula based on salary levels. This can be for one employee or every employee. For instance, a number of larger companies provide all employees who meet basic service requirements with 10% of pay every year in stock options. The argument behind such formulas is that salary reflects management's judgment of an employee's contributions to the company, and equity is simply another form of compensation.

Many companies provide awards on hiring, then make additional grants periodically or upon promotion. Linking additional grants to promotion gives employees an incentive to improve their skills and rewards those people the organization believes are making greater contributions. On the other hand, an overemphasis on promotion-related grants can mean that employees who are very good performers but who are not in jobs that can easily lead to a promotion are overlooked.

Refresher grants give employees additional awards when they exercise some of the options or other equity benefits they were previously granted. For instance, if an employee has 1,000 options on a capital or profits interest and exercises 200, then the employee would be given new options on another 200 shares at exercise. The theory here is to maintain a constant level of ownership interest in the company. Similarly, refresher awards might be granted when the company issues additional equity interests so that an employee maintains the same percentage of potential ownership as was held before the dilution. While these automatic additional grants help to keep the employee's equity interest high, other owners might object to the ongoing dilution.

How Often Should Awards Be Granted?

Equity inherently involves risk, but the design of plans can accentuate that risk. Companies that provide one-time grants of appreciation-based awards and grant them only upon an event, such as hiring, promotion, or meeting some corporate target, wind up with employees whose ownership interest in the company is based on the price of stock at a single point in time. This is not a problem with full-value awards, which do not have an exercise price based on the stock's trading price on the grant date.

Granting appreciation-based awards infrequently accelerates the risk of equity both for the employee and the company because equity granted at a high price may never be "in the money"; awards granted at a low price may cost the company more than it ever intended when the awards are redeemed. Employees who happen to receive their equity awards at a good time end up doing very well, while those who receive their grants when the price is not so favorable don't do well at all. Creating an ownership culture of "we're all in this together" can be very difficult in these circumstances.

For many companies, the best way to deal with these potential problems is to provide grants in smaller amounts but more frequently or to grant full-value awards such as restricted equity or phantom equity. Frequent grants work best for companies using equity as a compensation strategy. Startups whose equity value is close to zero or that use large initial grants to attract people away from other opportunities may find this less appropriate. It also is not appropriate for companies that want simply to make occasional grants at the discretion of the company, often on the attainment of some corporate milestone. These companies see equity more as a symbolic reward than as an ongoing ownership strategy.

The periodic allocation "dollar-cost averages" the awards, smoothing bumps in volatile markets. This approach also gives employees more of a long-term, ongoing stake in the company. With the vesting schedules attached to the repeated grants of awards, employees are provided an even longer-term interest in the company's performance. Finally, there will be fewer big winners and losers among employees with otherwise similar jobs.

Frequent grants are not all good news, of course. The more often awards are granted, the more complex their administration becomes. There is much more data entry, many more forms to file and disseminate, and many more errors that can be made. It may also become complicated because of frequent tax withholding and tax reporting.

When Will Employees Be Able to Use the Awards?

There are two principal issues in deciding when employees will be able to translate their equity into cash: vesting and exercise periods. Vesting generally provides that an employee accrues an increasing right to the awards granted based on the number of years worked. However, there is a growing use of performance vesting, in which vesting is a function of company, group, or individual performance. As various targets are met, the equity awards become increasingly vested. The exercise period is the time between an award's vesting and its expiration. Some types of awards may vest automatically upon exercise, especially equity-equivalent rights. Outright grants of capital or profits interests might vest at grant, but more commonly would have a vesting period. Once vested, there typically would be no further deferral of the actual receipt of the award.

Options present a different scenario. Here the employee might become fully vested in a right to acquire a profits or capital interest, but choose to defer it until later for tax or cash flow reasons. The most common exercise period for stock options in S or C corporations is ten years. Grants of restricted stock (stock that is tradable only after certain conditions, such as working for a defined period of time, are met) do not have an exercise period; instead, the restrictions lapse upon vesting, typically after three to five years. Given that many LLCs may have shorter time horizons than public companies (they may be working toward a sale or an initial public offering), they may want a shorter period in which an award can be exercised.

Vesting schedules are fairly consistent across companies, with three-to five-year graduated vesting the most common schedule. Sales, profit targets, and cash flow are the most common performance triggers. A few companies allow employees to exercise their awards only when a defined event occurs, such as the achievement of a certain stock price or earnings goal. This accomplishes two things. First, it provides an incentive to meet the goal, and second, it reassures investors that dilution will occur only if the company meets certain targets. Once these targets are met, employees are normally given a certain amount of time to exercise the award, anywhere from a few months to several years. Alternatively, a company could provide that awards can be exercised only upon the occurrence of an event, such as a sale or going public.

In closely held companies, allowing exercise of an award only upon sale of the company or an IPO is a very common approach. If an option is exercised or the company allows restricted stock to vest before then, employees end up owning stock and having a tax obligation. Unless the company can provide a market for the shares (an issue discussed below), this combination may not be perceived by the employee as much of a reward. Companies and employees must evaluate just how likely these events are to occur, however. Management is often excessively optimistic about how marketable the company is.

It is also important to consider that if equity compensation awards all become exercisable upon sale or an IPO, buyers of the stock may not find the company so valuable. A growing number of closely held companies are restricting exercise to sometime after a sale or an IPO (in a sale situation, this requires the acquiring company to provide options in the new employer) to ensure that there are adequate employee incentives in place following the sale or IPO.

Providing a Market for the Shares

Providing for liquidity of equity awards is one of the most important of all design issues. Most closely held companies solve the problem by limiting the exercise or sale of equity awards to when the company is sold or goes public. This makes sense for companies that realistically see these alternatives as likely to happen in the foreseeable future. Some company leaders, however, assume that they can provide for marketability only upon these events because a closely held company, for one reason or another, cannot provide a market itself. There are, in fact, alternatives for those companies and for companies that prefer to stay closely held and have no plans to sell or become public. These companies can provide an internal market by buying back the equity interests themselves or allowing other employees to buy them. This requires proper cash flow planning. Alternatively, an LLC could convert to a C or S corporation and set up an employee stock ownership plan (ESOP), which can buy the equity (now converted into shares) with pretax dollars through an ESOP trust.

Purchasing vs. Grant

A key consideration for many employers is whether employees should pay anything for their equity. At one extreme are employers in closely held companies who see the chance to own equity as itself a valuable benefit, even if it is offered at fair market value. At the other are those who believe employees cannot or should not take the risk to invest in company equity, but do want them to have a stake in the company. Several considerations apply to any choice on this matter:

• Do employees have the resources to buy equity? If not, is the company willing to lend them the money? If the loan carries an interest rate less than fair market value, there are possible tax implications with respect to the loan.

• How many employees will buy equity, either at full value or a discount? The results are often surprising and disappointing and may not provide enough people with an equity stake to accomplish the "ownership culture" objectives the company hopes to achieve.

• Even if many employees buy equity, will the distribution of ownership be enough to create a real stake in the outcome for most people? Employees whose financial obligations (or consumer preferences) leave them with little discretionary income, as well as employees who are risk-averse, may end up with only token amounts of equity.

• If there is a discount, how much will it be? Discounts may result in taxable income to the employee.

• Where options are issued, is paying for the exercise of an option good enough? If an employee uses cash or shares to exercise an option, is that enough to satisfy the company's desire to have people buy shares, even though there is a certain gain for those who sell their shares immediately?

In most companies, widespread ownership does not occur solely through an equity purchase plan. For some companies, however, broad ownership is not the goal. Rather, the objective is to engage specific employees and/or to raise capital. There is a perception that executives will have a greater interest in the company's success if they have some "skin in the game."

Perceptions vs. Reality

In classical economics, people are "rational" economic actors by definition. That means that they make choices about things based on maximizing their economic value. For instance, if people have the choice of having $1,000 now or a guaranteed $1,200 12 months from now, as rational actors, they would wait. It turns out that in reality this is not an accurate model of how people behave. Three notable characteristics are especially important for equity awards:

- *People overvalue current rewards:* Most people in the example above take the $1,000 now. They greatly undervalue the time value of money.

- *People value upside risk less than downside risk:* Researchers have asked people if they would make a double or nothing bet if they had lost $50. Most said yes. But if they had won $50 rather than losing $50, most said they would turn down a double or nothing bet. In the stock market, this helps explain why people hold on to losing shares too long.

- *People are willing to pay for perceived fairness:* In an often repeated experiment, people are asked to accept or not accept an offer to split $10 between them and someone else. If the split is $5/$5, everyone is happy, but if it is $7 and $3 or less, most people getting the $3 will say no—even though it means neither party gets anything.

An employee equity award works much the same way. The equity award will pay off only well into the future, carries uncertainty about how or if it will be paid for (because it will have liquidity only upon a sale or IPO), has some immediate tax consequences before the recipient is able to cash it in, and is granted to employees in ways that seem inconsistent with their value. All these factors greatly diminish the value of the award in the employees' eyes. As a result, the employer must dole out more than probably it wishes to provide the incentive effect sought. So while employers often want to design awards that seem most favorable to their liquidity, that reward only very long-term employees (even though most people are not sure when they receive the award if they will stay a long time), have no clear liquidity event, and have tax consequences that the employer does not cover, this "favorable" design may be a waste of equity. Similarly, if equity awards are perceived as unfair, employees who receive what they see as the short end of the stick will feel punished, not rewarded, even though the employer is giving them something extra. The employer will be in a worse position (in terms of employee attitudes) than if they had made no grants at all. Consequently, it is imperative in plan design to remember how people actually behave, not how they "should" behave.

Conclusion

Designing an effective equity plan is a difficult balancing act. There are no perfect approaches. The financial and organizational significance of these plans demands that they be considered at least as carefully as any other major investment of company assets and time, not just picked at random or based on limited information. Try to talk to peers who have set up plans (the NCEO can help its members identify other companies with plans), interview different consultants, read enough to feel comfortable with plan structures, and seek the input of board members and, preferably, employees about what kind of plan will work best—and be prepared to make changes as you learn more.

Chapter 3

Equity Interests in Limited Liability Companies

David R. Johanson, Rachel J. Markun, and Samuel W. Krause[1]

The limited liability company (LLC) is a form of business organization that may be used in all 50 states and the District of Columbia. LLCs have become increasingly popular because of their ability to provide limited liability protection without the partnership distinctions that apply to general partners and limited partners. LLCs are similar to corporations in that they provide owners with liability protection but are taxed as partnerships (unless the LLC elects to be taxed as a corporation). The operating agreement for the LLC should specifically define whether the LLC will be treated as a partnership or as a corporation for tax purposes. Because ownership in an LLC is evidenced by membership interests rather than capital stock, LLCs cannot sponsor employee stock ownership plans (ESOPs), grant stock options, provide restricted stock grants, or otherwise provide employees actual shares of capital stock or rights to purchase shares of capital stock; however, employees of an LLC that is in the same controlled group of corporations as a corporation that sponsors an ESOP may participate in an ESOP if the ESOP plan document so provides. But many LLCs want to reward employees with an equity stake in the company. The proper tax treatment of these equity interests to the recipient and the LLC and the mechanism for accom-

---

1.   Parts of this chapter were originally developed by Dan Janich of Greensfelder, Hemker & Gale, P.C., and Corey Rosen of the NCEO.

plishing grants of equity to LLC employees is not clear. For this reason, LLCs frequently face formidable challenges in providing employees with an equity interest in the company. This chapter explores the types of equity interests that an LLC can issue to its employees, the manner in which an LLC may provide such equity interests to its employees, and how such interests are treated for tax purposes.

LLCs in Brief

As in S corporations and partnerships, income from the operation of an LLC is attributed to the individual owners (referred to as "members"), who pay income tax on such income at personal tax rates.[2] Absent an election to the contrary in the operating agreement and with the Internal Revenue Service (IRS), single-member LLCs are taxed as disregarded entities, and multiple-member LLCs are taxed as partnerships. A disregarded entity's taxable items of income, deduction, gain, and loss are reported by its single member on that member's tax return (i.e., for individuals, a Form 1040). Unlike S corporations, LLCs are not required to allocate income and distributions to members exactly in proportion to their individual ownership interests, and an LLC may allocate such items in accordance with the terms of its operating agreement as long as such "special allocations" have economic substance as defined under the partnership tax rules. IRS rules governing income and distributions from LLCs are fairly complex, and thus LLC operations generally require guidance from experienced tax and legal advisors. Although the income taxation of equity interests that are issued by LLCs is complex, with good advice, these challenges should not in themselves be a sufficient reason for a business that is interested in issuing equity incentives to automatically switch to S corporation status.

Advantages and Disadvantages of LLCs vs. S Corporations

When determining whether an LLC should convert to an S corporation, the uncertainties of equity compensation in LLCs should be only one of

---

2. Note that an ESOP trust generally need not pay taxes on its share of income of an S corporation because it is a tax-exempt shareholder and there is no corporate level tax in an S corporation, subject to certain anti-abuse and concentration-of-equity requirements set forth in Section 409(p) of the Internal Revenue Code of 1986, as amended (the "Code").

many considerations to influence the decision. LLCs have a number of advantages over S corporations besides flexibility in specially allocating income and distributions:

- S corporations can have no more than 100 owners; there are no such ownership limitations for LLCs.

- Only individuals, certain trusts, and estates may own S corporation capital stock, but any entity, trust, estate, or individual may own an LLC interest, including a non-resident alien.

- LLC members are allocated a tax basis for the debt of the company, meaning losses can be passed through for more than what is invested by a member in circumstances where the member is personally liable for the debt repayment if the LLC defaults.

- LLCs may have multiple classes of ownership interests. S corporations may generally only have one class of capital stock; however, an S corporation may have both voting and non-voting common stock. Wholly owned subsidiaries may have their assets, liabilities, and profits treated separately from the LLC.

- LLCs are often used to move assets around in tax-favored ways, such as gifting interests to heirs without providing any control rights or moving appreciated property into an LLC for greater limitation of liability protection without tax consequences. In a corporation, once the assets are taken out, there is a taxable gain.

- LLCs may usually be readily converted to S or C corporation status.

- Some states have entity-level taxes on S corporations but not on LLCs.

- LLCs generally do not have the same obligations as S or C corporations to keep board of director meeting minutes or require shareholder resolutions, and they otherwise have fewer compliance burdens than S or C corporations.

- LLCs may provide a profits interest to a service provider or consultant tax-free, whereas receipt of an unrestricted stock interest in an S corporation by a service provider or consultant results in taxable income on its fair market value upon receipt.

LLCs also have a number of disadvantages compared to S corporations:

• Unlike the case with S or C corporations, if an LLC is purchased by another company, it is more difficult to complete a tax-free combination.

• Profits in an S corporation that are distributed to shareholder-employees may avoid some self-employment taxes (FICA and FUTA), whereas self-employment taxes on such profits in an LLC may be unavoidable for certain employees.

• LLCs are relatively recent creatures of state law, so the kind of developed, relatively uniform corporate law guidance that exists for S or C corporations is not available for LLC governance matters.

• Amounts attributable to inventory and accounts receivable in an LLC are taxed as ordinary income upon sale of the company; in an S corporation, they are taxed as capital gains.

• Many venture capital firms, because of restrictions imposed by their pension or retirement trust fund clients, cannot invest in LLCs because of the application of the unrelated business income tax (UBIT) to such investments. This is not the case with private equity firms, however, many of which are structured as LLCs.

Purchases or Gifts of Equity Interests in LLCs

The simplest approach is to have employees purchase an equity interest in the company. The question here is whether this really is an equity incentive rather than simply an employee investment. It may depend on the purchase price. Some companies see the opportunity to buy ownership as an incentive, but many, if not most, employees will either not have the resources to make the investment, will decide other investments are more appropriate for them, or will have expectations resulting from the investment, such as a say in how the company is managed, that the other members may not want to cede. Alternatively, employees can be granted an equity interest, but some owners think that unless employees have "skin in the game," they will not really act like owners (although evidence of this is unclear).

General Considerations When Providing Employee Ownership to Employees of LLCs

It is important to remember when considering any of the following approaches that because an LLC is taxed as a partnership, a member is treated as a partner, rather than an employee, for federal tax purposes. The IRS has proposed regulations under Section 742 of the Code that address whether a member in an LLC is treated as a general partner or a limited partner for tax purposes. Under these proposed regulations, if a member may enter into contracts on behalf of the LLC, he or she will be deemed a general partner for tax purposes. If the member is a general partner, such member (1) will receive a Schedule K-1, rather than a Form W-2 from the LLC; (2) will have his or her "salary" taxed as a "guaranteed payment" under Code Section 707(c); (3) will not have income taxes withheld by the LLC; (4) will not have employment taxes (including FUTA) paid or withheld on his/her behalf by the LLC; (5) will not be able to collect unemployment benefits; (6) will have to pay estimated taxes quarterly; and (7) will have to pay self-employment taxes of up to 15.3% (16.2% starting in 2013) on self-employment income from the LLC.

Types of Equity Interests Available in LLCs

Where the company wants to award ownership interests to an employee of an LLC, there are two primary types of equity interests available:

1. *Capital interests* give the owner a right to share in the value of LLC assets through the receipt of a share of the proceeds upon sale of the LLC assets, and the proceeds of the sale are distributed in a complete liquidation of the LLC.

    Example 1: ABC LLC has three existing members, Able, Bill, and Charlie, each with a capital account of $500, which also constitutes the $1,500 fair market value of the assets of ABC LLC. ABC LLC has an employee, Don, whom it admits as a member of LLC, with a 5% capital interest in ABC LLC. Assuming that upon his admittance as a member Don does not contribute any additional funds to ABC LLC or otherwise pay for his capital interest, the capital interest effectively entitles Don to $75 (5% of $1,500) if ABC LLC were immediately liquidated. Able, Bill, and Charlie would now each have a capital account of $475. They will have been diluted by sharing equity in the LLC with Don.

2. *Profits interests* entitle the owner both to capital appreciation and profits of the business, providing the holder with a share in the profits of the LLC and a right to share in any increase in the fair market value of the LLC. Therefore, if the LLC were to be immediately liquidated on the date of grant, the recipient of the profits interest would not be entitled to any distribution on his or her profits interest; if liquidation is later, as would normally be the case, the holder can receive both a share of profits and appreciation, as in the example below.

   Example 2: Assume the same facts as in example 1, except that now Don receives a grant of a 5% profits interest in the LLC, which entitles him to 5% of all future profits of ABC LLC, and 5% of the future growth in fair market value in excess of the fair market value of the assets of ABC LLC at the date of grant of the profits interest ($1,500). Assuming that ABC LLC distributes profits in each of the next two years of $100 per year, Don would receive distributions of $5 each year (5% of $100). Also, if ABC LLC is then sold at a time when the fair market value of the LLC is $2,000, Don would be entitled to $25 ($2,000 - $1,500 = $500, multiplied by 5% = $25).

Either type of interest may be subject to restrictions, such as a vesting requirement that is satisfied by the employee's service for a specified period of time or by satisfaction of certain performance standards. Either type of interest may be forfeited if the employee engages in criminal activity that results in direct harm to the company, such as embezzlement. Many companies also will want employees to forfeit their capital and/or profits interests if they go to work for competitors. While these anti-competition agreements can be written into equity grant agreements, they may be difficult to enforce. Many companies choose to take a middle ground, writing into their equity grant agreements repurchase rights and rights of first refusal that allow the LLC to buy back the employee's interest in the event that they leave the LLC, coupled with more limited "forfeiture" rights with respect to an employee who has been terminated by the LLC for "cause" as defined in the LLC's operating agreement. There can be variations as well in which the purchase price of the equity is modified based upon the circumstances and timing of the termination of the LLC employee who previously received a grant of equity. Whereas repurchase rights and rights of first refusal generally provide for a selling employee to receive the fair market value or book value of his or her capital interest, the "forfeiture" provisions often provide for the "bad actor" terminated employee to receive the lesser of fair market value or what he or she paid, if anything, to acquire the equity interest in the LLC. Either way, when structuring such arrangements, it is important to consider how the valuation and purchase price will be established (such as by a fixed formula, an independent appraisal, or otherwise). The use of an independent appraiser (albeit fairly expensive) adds some significant credibility to an equity incentive plan as employee participants now know that an independent third party establishes the fair market value of their equity. Furthermore, it is not uncommon to couple such arrangements with noncompetition, nondisclosure, nonsolicitation, and nondisparagement arrangements.

The grant of either a capital or profits equity interest in an LLC is a contractual matter. LLCs need to have a written plan under which grants, awards, or purchases can be provided, as well as individual agreements with employees detailing each party's rights and obligations, and these agreements need to comport not only with state and federal law but also with the LLC's formation and operating agreements. Because of the myriad of considerations involved, it is essential that these documents be developed by qualified legal counsel and that they define all terms and requirements unambiguously. Furthermore, as a general matter, the grant of a capital equity interest typically requires a valuation of the LLC as of the date of grant, award, or purchase to establish a benchmark against which the future increase in the fair market value of the LLC may be measured.

As noted in the previous chapter, another form of compensation that is common to many LLCs (particularly private equity and hedge funds) is the "carried interest," a perceived form of equity. Essentially, a carried interest is a profits interest. Although the carried interest is not actually equity in the LLC, it can be designed in a manner that provides the holder with an ongoing right to future income, which can be sold or otherwise transferred to others, depending on its terms and the operating agreement of the LLC.

Tax Consequences of Granting a Capital Interest in an LLC

An employee who receives an equity capital interest that is freely transferrable or without a substantial risk of forfeiture (that is, a vested capital interest) in an LLC in exchange for services rendered[3] recognizes ordinary compensation income (at ordinary income tax rates of taxation) in an amount equal to the fair market value of the equity capital interest less the amount, if any, paid for the interest. The fair market value of such an interest received as compensation for personal services must generally be included in the recipient's gross income in the first tax year in which the member may transfer the equity capital interest or the interest is not subject to a substantial risk of forfeiture. The fair market value of this interest, for purposes of computing the employee's income and the LLC's deduction, may be determined in one of several ways: (1) by reference to the fair market value of the personal services rendered to the fair market value of the LLC's assets; (2) by determining the value of the capital that was shifted from existing LLC members to the new grantee;[4] (3) by determining the fair market value according to what a willing buyer and willing seller would agree upon as a purchase price in an arm's-length sale (i.e., the willing buyer/willing seller test); or (4) by determining the amount that the employee would receive upon a liquidation of the LLC at the time the interest is issued (i.e., the liquidation value). Regardless of the method used to determine fair market value, income and employment tax withholding will be required.

> *Example 3:* ABC LLC has three existing members, Able, Bill, and Charlie, each with a capital account of $500, and which constitutes the $1,500 fair market value of the assets of ABC LLC. ABC LLC has

---

3.   Although it also is possible to make the same type of grant for personal services to be rendered by the employee, rather than those already rendered, it is unlikely that such a grant would be made free of some vesting restrictions that would constitute a substantial risk of forfeiture.

4.   An LLC will frequently "revalue" its assets immediately before the grant of a capital interest to a new member to prevent a "capital shift" of pregrant appreciation of LLC assets in favor of the grantee. A shift in an LLC member's share of company liabilities would result in an increase in basis for the new owner's membership interest in the LLC.

an employee, Don, which it admits as a member of the LLC, with a 5% equity capital interest in ABC LLC. The grant to Don is fully vested, not otherwise subject to a substantial risk of forfeiture, and is being made in exchange for personal services rendered by Don to ABC LLC. Assuming upon his admittance as a member that Don does not contribute any additional funds to ABC LLC or otherwise pay for his equity capital interest, and the fair market value of the personal services rendered by Don to ABC LLC for which he is receiving the equity capital interest is $100 (established based on pay actually given up by Don in consideration for the grant), Don would be taxed at ordinary income tax rates on $100 of income in the year the grant is made (unless the grant of equity is not freely transferrable or is subject to a substantial risk of forfeiture), and ABC LLC would be entitled to a $100 deduction for this same period.

Example 4: Assuming the same facts as in example 3, except that the fair market value of the personal services rendered by Don to ABC LLC is not easily established. Prior to the grant of Don's equity capital interest, each of the members of ABC LLC (Able, Bill, and Charlie) is entitled to one-third of ABC LLC upon a sale and distribution of the proceeds therefrom. Also assume that ABC LLC is valued at $1,800 immediately before the grant of the equity capital interest to Don, so the fair market value of each of Able, Bill, and Charlie's equity capital interests in ABC LLC would be $600. After the grant of Don's equity capital interest to Don, the fair market value of Able, Bill, and Charlie's capital interests would be $570 each. This represents a total capital shift of $90 ($30 multiplied by 3 = $90) from Able, Bill, and Charlie to Don. Therefore, Don would be taxed at ordinary income tax rates on $90 of income in the year the grant is made (unless the grant of equity is not freely transferrable or is subject to a substantial risk of forfeiture), and ABC LLC would be entitled to a $90 deduction for this same period.

Example 5: Assuming the same facts as in example 4, except that at the same time as Don is granted his capital interest of 5% in ABC LLC, Ed purchases a 10% capital interest in ABC LLC for $250. Using the fair market value of Ed's purchase of a capital interest in the LLC as a guide, Don's capital interest would be valued at $125

($250 multiplied by 50%). Therefore, Don would be taxed at ordinary income tax rates on $125 of income in the year the grant is made (unless the grant of equity is not freely transferable or is subject to a substantial risk of forfeiture), and ABC LLC would be entitled to a $125 deduction for this same period.

Example 6: Assuming the same facts as in example 3, the capital interest effectively entitles Don to $75 (5% of $1,500) if ABC LLC were immediately liquidated. Able, Bill, and Charlie would now each have a capital account of $475. Therefore, Don would be taxed at ordinary income tax rates on $75 of income in the year the grant is made (unless the grant of equity is not freely transferrable or is subject to a substantial risk of forfeiture), and ABC LLC would be entitled to a $75 deduction for this same period.

If the interest is subject to a substantial risk of forfeiture and is nontransferable, then the taxable event can be delayed until the restriction lapses unless the employee makes a Code Section 83(b) election. A Code Section 83(b) election must be made by the employee within 30 days of the grant's award. The election states that the employee agrees to be taxed immediately upon receipt of the capital interest at ordinary income rates, with any subsequent appreciation in the interest taxed at capital gain rates upon disposition. A Code Section 83(b) election may be made where there is no bargain element in the equity purchase or grant and no gain (for example, where an interest in an LLC worth $100 is purchased for $100 as well as where there is taxable gain to report). An employee who receives a restricted capital interest will not be treated as a partner for tax purposes until the restrictions lapse unless the Code Section 83(b) election is made. Furthermore, if a Code Section 83(b) election is made, and the employee later forfeits all or part of the award, the employee is not entitled to a refund with respect to the income taxes he or she already paid.

If a Code Section 83(b) election is not made, then ordinary income tax is paid on the fair market value of the award at the time it vests (i.e., when the equity is freely transferable or no longer subject to a substantial risk of forfeiture). Please note that this is not the same as when the employee actually sells the capital interest, which may be later. Any difference between the price at vesting and the price at sale would be subject to long- or short-term capital gains taxes, depending on how long the LLC employee holds the capital interest.

The LLC is entitled to a deduction for the fair market value of the capital interest that the employee reported as income at vesting or upon the employee making the Code Section 83(b) election, and the LLC has the obligation to withhold income and employment taxes, as with any employee compensation. Despite the fact that the capital interest is being exchanged for the employee's services, there is a risk that the LLC may still be required to recognize gain for a "deemed sale" consisting of the sale of an interest in its assets for cash, payment of the cash to the employee who rendered services to the LLC, and a subsequent contribution of the cash by the employee back to the LLC in exchange for the capital interest. Any gain resulting from the deemed sale would be taxable to the other LLC members but offset in part by a deduction for compensation paid to the employee.

Tax Consequences of Granting a Profits Interest in an LLC

Under IRS Revenue Procedure 93-27 and IRS Revenue Procedure 2001-43, if a person receives a profits interest for the provision of services to or for the benefit of an LLC, in a membership capacity or in anticipation of being a member, the IRS will not treat the receipt of such an interest as a taxable event for the member or the LLC. Revenue Procedure 93-27 includes an IRS-provided safe harbor, providing that an employee's receipt of a profits interest in exchange for services is not taxable upon grant, even if the interest is fully vested, if each of the following requirements are satisfied:

1. The interest is not sold within two years of receipt.

2. The receipt of a profits interest is not related to a substantially certain and predictable stream of income (such as income from high-quality debt securities or a high-quality net lease).[5]

---

5.   The safe harbor provided in Revenue Procedure 93-27 includes a third requirement that is not applicable to LLCs: that if the profits interest is a limited partnership interest, it may not be an interest in a "publicly traded partnership."

In 2001, the IRS issued Revenue Procedure 2001-43, which clarifies Revenue Procedure 93-27 by providing that the determination under Revenue Procedure 93-27 of whether an interest granted to a service provider is a profits interest is tested at the time the interest is granted, even if, at that time, the interest is unvested. Under this guidance, where an LLC grants a profits interest to an employee, the IRS will not treat the grant of the interest, or the vesting of the interest, as a taxable event for the employee or the LLC if the following requirements are met:

1. The LLC and the employee treat the employee as the tax owner of the interest from the date of its grant, and the employee reports his or her distributive share of all partnership tax items in computing the employee's income tax liability for the entire period during which the employee has the interest.

2. Upon the grant of the interest or at the time that the interest vests, neither the LLC nor any of its members deducts any amount (as wages, compensation, or otherwise) for the fair market value of the interest.

3. The conditions of Revenue Procedure 93-27 are satisfied. [6]

Therefore, under Revenue Procedure 2001-43, if the grant of a profits interest satisfies the requirements discussed above, the tax consequences of the grant of the profits interest are:

1. No income or employment taxes are owed by the employee.

2. The LLC does not have any obligation to withhold income taxes.

3. The LLC is not entitled to take a compensation deduction in the year in which the employee includes the amount in income.

4. The employee is entitled to capital gains treatment with respect to the subsequent redemption or sale of the profits interest.

---

6.   In May 2005, the IRS issued Notice 2005-43 and proposed Treasury regulations that would make Revenue Procedure 93-27 and Revenue Procedure 2001-43 obsolete. Until the new rules are finalized (which has not happened as of this writing), Revenue Procedure 93-27 and Revenue Procedure 2001-43 will continue to apply.

5.   The employee does need not file an election under Section 83(b) of the Code.

If the safe harbor requirements are not satisfied, there is some un-certainty as to the employee's income tax consequences arising from the grant of a profits interest to an employee, so the grants tend to be based on the safe harbor standards.

Where the profits interest is not vested at the time of grant, the employee will not be considered as the owner of the interest until it is fully vested unless a Code Section 83(b) election is made or the employee is treated as having made such an election (see below). If the employee cannot be treated as the owner of the interest, then the employee cannot be allocated profits or losses of the LLC until the interest vests. Once vested, however, the employee would be entitled to receive appreciation on the property for the period running between grant of the interest and its vesting unless there is an adjustment that allocates the built-in appreciation to existing members instead. It is worth noting that the receipt of an allocation of existing appreciation at the time of grant may convert the profits interest into a capital interest that is taxable at the time of vesting.

When the employee does redeem the profits interest, the gain is taxed as either short- or long-term capital gain.

How an employee should deal with making a Code Section 83(b) election is not entirely resolved, particularly in light of the IRS safe harbor, which allows for receipt of a vested profits interest to escape tax. IRS guidance has indicated that a restricted profits interest would be treated as received on the grant date rather than the vesting date if the recipient is treated as owner of the interest (receiving a distributive share of LLC items attributable to the interest) and the LLC does not claim a tax deduction for the fair market value of the interest in the year it was granted or in the year in which it vests. In other words, the profits interest is treated as if a Code Section 83(b) election were made. As a result of this further guidance, there may no longer be a need to file a Code Section 83(b) election to include in the current year's income the fair market value of a restricted profit interest, although most advisors would urge that an election be made anyway to protect against some unforeseen circumstance making this treatment inapplicable.

Furthermore, profits interest holders must receive a Schedule K-1 statement attributing their respective share of ownership to them, and they must pay estimated income taxes on all income from the LLC (as well as self-employment taxes on their salary from the LLC). That means they will have a tax responsibility for the current income or gains of the LLC even though vesting rules for the award of LLC distribution policies do not entitle them to any distributions with which to pay these taxes. In an S corporation, distributions must be made pro-rata to owners, but, as noted above, this is not true in an LLC, so the LLC is not obligated to make sure the profits interest holder receives a distribution sufficient to pay taxes. Profits interest holders, of course, will want these "tax distributions." If they are paid, then such tax distributions would be treated as advances against any future distributions to which the profits interest holder would be entitled. The special allocations rules may ease this burden such that the distributions of gain to the profits holder is deferred until there is income to distribute.

Employees with profits interests are taxed as partners rather than employees, so their entire income is reported on a Schedule K-1 and is not subject to withholding. Holders must pay estimated income taxes on all their income from the LLC and self-employment taxes on salary.

Because a carried interest is the equivalent of a profits interest in the LLC, it has the same tax ramifications as the profits interest as discussed above. It should be noted that some LLCs use the term "carried interest," but in reality they are simply providing bonuses to employees. Each situation should be separately evaluated to determine whether the employee actually has a profits interest in the LLC.

Options to Acquire a Capital Interest or Profits Interest

As stated previously, there are two types of equity interests available in LLCs. As an alternative to the grant of an outright interest, LLCs may issue options to acquire either a capital interest or a profits interest. The advantage in doing so is that the grant of an option in such case is not taxable to the employee or to the LLC. An employee who exercises an option acquires an immediate interest in the underlying assets and future revenues of the LLC if the option includes the right to acquire a capital interest and a profits interest in the LLC.

The exercise of an option on a capital interest will result in taxable income for the employee and a deduction for the LLC. The amount of taxable income equals the excess of the fair market value of the LLC interest received over the exercise price, if any, and the LLC would get a corresponding tax deduction for this amount. At exercise, the LLC would also need to address the "deemed sale" issue discussed previously. These tax consequences can be delayed with restrictions on transferability or substantial risks of forfeiture.

The exercise of an option on a profits interest would not be taxable for the employee or LLC if the safe harbor rules are satisfied. At exercise, the appreciation in fair market value issue discussed above would also need to be addressed.

Phantom Equity or Performance Shares

For some of the reasons discussed above, as well a myriad of other reasons, many companies are uncomfortable with issuing equity to employees. One possible solution to this problem is the use of "phantom equity" or "performance shares." The use of phantom equity or performance shares allows an LLC to provide an employee a contractual right to receive additional income from the company that looks and feels like equity but in fact is a cash bonus that will be taxed as ordinary income upon receipt. Such arrangements allow the employee to participate in the financial rewards of ownership (such as an appreciation in the fair market value of the LLC for a particular period of time) without having voting and other ownership rights usually associated with true equity.

Phantom equity or performance share arrangements are extremely flexible, can be structured in a variety of different ways, and are essentially just cash bonus plans under which the bonus amount (usually subject to vesting) is calculated using a formula related to the LLC's financial results or increase in fair market value of the LLC. The formula employed by a company in creating a phantom equity plan or performance share arrangement can be structured virtually any way that the company determines is appropriate for the equity holder. For example, the formula could be (1) based on how much the book value or fair market value of the LLC increases (before vesting) following the award of the phantom equity or performance shares by the LLC; (2) based upon the book value or fair market value of a certain percentage of the LLC on a given vesting date; or (3) based on the profits achieved by the LLC over a specified period (e.g., an "account" to which the LLC credits a percentage of its profits, the proceeds of which are distributed to the employee if he or she remains with the company for five years). These are just a few of the many creative examples that exist.

Phantom equity plans and performance share arrangements that are set up and administered correctly in accordance with the Code Section 409A rules described below are taxed in the same manner as any other nonqualified deferred compensation plan: the employee is subject to ordinary income tax and the LLC is entitled to a tax deduction only when the employee actually receives payments under the plan or arrangement. It is important to remember that, as with all deferred compensation, such a result can be achieved with respect to phantom plans or arrangements only with careful planning, documentation, and administration.

Impact of Section 409A on Equity Interests in LLCs

Section 409A of the Code requires deferred compensation plans to comply with various rules that are designed to place reasonable operational limits on the timing of an election to defer income as well as the events that entitle a participant to receive a plan distribution. This provision was enacted in response to perceived abuses in deferred compensation arrangements that had allowed many executives to determine the timing and form of payment from these plans. As a result of the enactment of Code Section 409A, virtually any plan, arrangement, or agreement that defers income tax on compensation is subject to its stringent requirements.

A failure to comply with either documentation or operational requirements of Code Section 409A results in immediate income taxation on amounts previously deferred by plan participants as well as the assessment of 20% excise taxes and late payment interest. Although the IRS provides a procedure for correcting inadvertent operational errors, which generally involve either deferred amounts that should have been paid or amounts that should have been deferred, this is definitely a situation where an ounce of prevention is worth a pound of cure.[7]

Although IRS Notice 2005-1[8] does not specifically mention LLCs, it states that Code Section 409A "is not limited to arrangements between an employer and employee" and "may apply to arrangements between a partner and a partnership which provides for the deferral of compensation under a nonqualified deferral compensation plan." The reference to partnerships also should apply to LLCs taxable as partnerships.

It is essential that careful analysis be undertaken to distinguish between payments of compensation made by an LLC to an employee who is not a member of the LLC, the transfer of a membership interest in the LLC as compensation to an employee, a distribution made to a member with respect to his or her membership interest, and a payment of compensation for services to a member that is not a distribution with respect to his or her membership interest (for example, a "guaranteed payment" under Code Section 707(c)). Payments made by an LLC to an employee and payments made to a member that are not distributions with respect to such member's ownership interest in the LLC are treated analogously to payments received from a C corporation; therefore, they generally are analyzed under Code Section 409A with respect to the same rules that apply to C corporations. As a result, IRS Notice 2005-1 may be interpreted to permit taxpayers to treat the issuance of an equity interest (including a profits interest), or an option to purchase an equity interest, granted by an LLC in connection with the performance of services, under the same principles that govern the issuance of stock under Code Section 409A. A closer look at how such interests would be treated for Code Section 409A purposes follows.

---

7.   The current version of this program appears in IRS Notice 2008-113.

8.   Section III.G of the preamble to the final regulations under Section 409A states that Notice 2005-1 continues to provide interim guidance regarding the application of Section 409A until further guidance is issued. There are many unresolved issues with respect to the application of Section 409A to transfers of compensatory interests in LLCs. Until further guidance is issued, LLCs should strive to structure their equity arrangements to comply with Section 409A to the greatest extent possible.

Restricted and Unrestricted Capital Interests

In the context of LLC interests, IRS Notice 2005-1 would permit the issuance of a compensatory capital interest to be treated in the same manner as the issuance of capital stock, i.e., not resulting in the deferral of compensation because its value (and any subsequent income earned in respect of the capital interest) would be included in the recipient's income upon issuance. As such, the issuance and holding of a compensatory capital interest would be excluded from Code Section 409A's requirements. The receipt of a restricted capital interest (typically, one subject to a vesting schedule) is not a taxable event at the time of transfer (unless a Code Section 83(b) election has been made by the recipient). It may be appropriate for Code Section 409A to apply to a transfer of a compensatory restricted capital interest, or a promise to deliver a capital interest in the future, where such interest or promise is not contingent on the performance of substantial future services, if the transfer or promise is considered to be a form of deferred compensation.

Profits Interests

IRS Notice 2005-1 specifically exempts profits interests from Code Section 409A if the recipient of the profits interest is not required to include the value of the interest in income at the time of issuance under applicable guidance. Current tax guidance provides that neither the receipt nor vesting of a compensatory profits interest is a taxable event.[9] Given that no income is recognized, none can be deferred under Code Section 409A.[10]

LLC Options to Acquire Capital or Profits Interest and Equity Appreciation Rights

IRS Notice 2005-1 provides that the treatment of compensatory issuances of LLC-based awards other than capital or profits interests may be governed, by analogy, under the Code Section 409A rules covering

---

9. Once vested, the service provider recognizes income on his or her allocable share of the LLC's future income when earned.

10. Current rules do not address exemption of a profits interest from Section 409A where the profits interest has a readily ascertainable value at the time of grant.

equity-based awards. Thus, the treatment of LLC options to acquire a capital or profits interest can be determined by reference to Code Section 409A's treatment of nonqualified stock options, and the treatment of LLC appreciation rights can be determined by reference to Code Section 409A's treatment of stock appreciation rights.

LLC Options to Acquire Capital or Profits Interest

IRS Notice 2005-1 states that the grant of a nonqualified stock option with respect to stock of a service recipient does not result in a deferral of compensation, and therefore avoids Code Section 409A, only if (1) the option exercise price is never less than the fair market value of the underlying stock on the grant date; (2) the receipt, transfer, or exercise of the option is subject to taxation under Code Section 83; and (3) the option does not include any additional deferral features. It may be impractical in certain circumstances to value LLC assets in connection with each option grant, due to the intangible or illiquid nature of the assets or equity involved. For this reason, an LLC interested in issuing option grants may wish to do so when other valuation events occur.

If the Code Section 409A requirements applicable to nonqualified stock options are not satisfied with respect to an option to acquire an LLC capital or profits interest, the option holder would likely recognize income upon option vesting equal to the excess of the fair market value of the LLC interest underlying the option over the amount of the exercise price, plus the additional 20% tax with interest under Code Section 409A.

LLC Equity Appreciation Rights

IRS Notice 2005-1 provides that stock appreciation rights are treated as deferral compensation subject to Code Section 409A unless (1) the rights relate to the stock of a service recipient, (2) the exercise price of the right is equal to fair market value of the stock on the date of grant, (3) the right settles only in stock, (4) the stock is traded on an established securities exchange, and (5) the right does not contain any additional deferral features. Using the foregoing criteria, LLC appreciation rights granted by most closely held LLCs would be subject to Code Section 409A because such LLC appreciation rights could not satisfy the "publicly traded" requirement.

It is possible for an LLC appreciation right to comply with Code Section 409A's requirements if the exercise date of such an appreciation right is fixed as of the grant date. In such a case, the appreciation right may provide that exercise will occur on the earlier of a date certain or termination of the LLC's employee's employment.

Earned Income and Availability of Tax-Favored Fringe Benefits

Not all LLC members may be treated for income tax purposes as common law employees. As such, only LLC members who are providing a service to the company, and thus receive earned income, may—but not always will—be considered for tax-favored treatment with respect to the company's benefit programs.

For example, under Revenue Ruling 91-26, premiums that an LLC pays for health insurance for its members are treated as guaranteed payments. The member/employee must report these premiums as income on his or her tax return but may take the corresponding deduction, permitted under Code Section 162(l), for the amount of the premiums for income tax (but not self-employment tax) purposes. Members who are compensated for services through guaranteed payments, considered to be earned income, will qualify to deduct 100% of their health insurance premiums to the extent of their pro-rata share of net profits.[11] The members' share of net profits is not considered earned income, and therefore inactive members who receive solely a distribution of profits will not qualify for the health insurance premium deduction.

The following fringe benefits also are excluded from employee compensation, but not from the income of self-employed a member/employee of an LLC: (1) up to $50,000 of group term life insurance;[12] (2) benefits received under a cafeteria plan;[13] (3) qualified transporta-

---

11. Guaranteed payments are defined in Treas. Reg. § 1.707-1(c) and are understood as "payments made by a partnership to a partner for services." As such, these payments are treated as self-employment income and therefore render the recipient eligible for deduction of his or her self-employed health insurance expenses.

12. Code Section 79.

13. Code Section 125.

tion fringe benefits (such as transit passes and paid parking);[14] and (4) lodging and meals furnished for the convenience of the LLC.[15]

Other Considerations

When deciding whether to grant equity compensation to an employee, the following additional issues may be considered (depending on the requirements of state law):

• Profits interests may be, and often are, structured as a new class of unit in the LLC. Employees who hold units generally are not required to share in guaranty obligations and make additional capital contributions.

• Capital interests granted to employees may be structured as a different class of units than those granted to founders.

• Units granted to employees may have full voting rights (including the right to participate in the election of managers), may have limited voting rights (i.e., only with respect to decisions regarding a merger of the LLC or a sale of substantially all of its assets) or may have no voting rights at all.

• Employees who hold units and do not have voting rights may still be entitled to attend members' meetings and participate in any discussions at such meetings, subject to the terms of the LLC's operating agreement.

It also is important to remember that when an employee becomes a member of the LLC, the operating agreement may need to be modified to address, among others: (1) any wage rights that the service provider is entitled to independently of the LLC interest; (2) any right that the LLC has to terminate the services of the service provider, and which member (or members) can exercise such right(s); (3) any residual rights that the service provider will have upon termination of employment; and (4) what happens to the membership interest of the service provider upon

---

14. Code Section 132(f).
15. Code Section 119.

termination of employment with the LLC (such as buy-sell provisions). Applicable state law should be considered before any of the foregoing is addressed with changes to the LLC's operating agreement.

Expert Advice Required

Because of their relative flexibility, LLCs may develop equity plans that fit their business objectives and align the interests of employees with the company to promote further growth of the enterprise. If designed to be taxed at capital gain rates, the capital interest or profits interest may provide the incentive needed for employees while minimizing dilution of ownership in the company. The limited guidance issued in this area poses unique challenges that must be handled with skill by an experienced advisor. Best practices are still evolving.

While it is always important to have expert advice regarding any equity plan, the complexity of the tax treatment that equity incentives in LLCs involve, as well as the more difficult planning issues, makes it even more important to engage people (tax experts and legal counsel) who know the field very well.

Chapter 4

Accounting for Equity Compensation in an LLC

Alan Nadel

The limited liability company (LLC) has become a common form of business organization in the U.S. only within the past 25 years. While those who establish accounting standards have paid much attention to equity compensation, their focus has been primarily on corporations rather than other forms of legal entities, such as LLCs and partnerships. It has been quite common for decades to provide equity interests to employees, particularly executives, as a means of providing incentive and long-term compensation. Because LLCs have been introduced only recently, the accounting literature applicable to equity compensation does not specifically address these types of entities. Nevertheless, the general language of the relevant accounting literature makes clear that it is appropriate to apply the same equity compensation accounting rules to other entities as those applicable to corporations.

Before getting into the specific rules applicable to equity compensation, it is first important to identify which set of rules we should be looking to. In the U.S., accounting for business transactions is covered under generally accepted accounting principles (GAAP). Virtually any transaction in American business is specifically addressed by one (and sometimes more than one) of the GAAP rules, including those for executive and employee pay programs. GAAP guidelines are developed primarily by the Financial Accounting Standards Board (FASB). All companies in the U.S. must follow GAAP regardless of whether they are publicly traded.

The FASB derives its authority from the Sarbanes-Oxley Act and the Securities and Exchange Commission (SEC). It is an independent board, but receives significant input from the SEC. Outside the U.S., accounting rules generally are established by the International Accounting Standards Board (IASB). The IASB establishes international financial reporting standards (IFRS) that have been adopted in more than 100 countries around the world. There has been considerable discussion in the U.S. about transitioning U.S. accounting standards from GAAP to IFRS within the next few years, but when and how this change will occur remains uncertain. Until a changeover to IFRS occurs, U.S. companies continue to be subject to the rules of GAAP; therefore, this discussion of relevant accounting principles will fall under the rules of GAAP. It should be noted, however, that while the rules of IFRS are similar to those of GAAP, notable differences exist between the two and may affect company stock-based programs if the U.S. eventually moves to IFRS.

Before 1995, the applicable accounting rules for equity compensation in the U.S. were dictated by Accounting Principles Board Opinion No. 25, *Accounting for Stock Issued to Employees* ("APB 25"). Recognizing that those accounting rules were developed for the simpler equity compensation programs of the early 1970s, the FASB decided to develop more comprehensive rules for equity compensation programs. It issued Statement of Financial Accounting Standards No. 123, *Accounting for Stock-Based Compensation* ("FAS 123"), in 1995. Under pressure from the business community, however, the FASB drafted FAS 123 to allow employers to choose whether they used the accounting of APB 25 or FAS 123. Most companies chose to continue using the older accounting rules under APB 25, whereby no expense was recognized for most stock options, and simply disclose the effect of FAS 123 in the financial statement footnotes. When the economic environment changed significantly, the FASB revised the 1995 rules and made them mandatory for all companies under rules issued in late 2004, Statement of Financial Accounting Standards No. 123 (revised 2004), *Share-Based Payment* ("FAS 123R"). In 2009, the FASB introduced a new codified system for accounting standards. The portions of FAS 123R relating to equity payments for employees became Accounting Standards Codification Topic 718 ("ASC 718"), and the parts of FAS 123R relating to nonemployees became Accounting Standards Codification Subtopic 505-50 ("ASC 505-50").

Applicable Accounting

The rules of ASC 718 make significant changes to the accounting practices that almost all companies were following until 2005. Unlike the intrinsic value rules of APB 25, ASC 718 requires that the "fair value" of all equity compensation awards be recognized as an expense. The rules of ASC 718 are different from those under current GAAP for recognizing the cost of other assets and liabilities. Some of these changes are:

- Use of special valuation models for determining the cost of employee options to purchase employer equity

- Accrual patterns for recognizing the expense associated with vested awards

- Recognition of the income tax effects of equity awards

- Impact of performance-vested awards

- Modifications and other changes to outstanding equity awards

Although the rules of ASC 718 are geared toward corporate stock programs, they are just as relevant for equity interests that are granted to employees of unincorporated entities, including LLCs. Not surprisingly, certain adjustments must be made. In some LLC companies, employees are allowed to purchase an equity interest in the LLC. If the cost of that capital interest in the LLC is on the same terms (e.g., price) as for other investors in the LLC, then the employee's acquisition of the capital interest likely would not be treated as a compensatory one. ASC 718 would not be applicable, and the LLC would recognize no compensation expense. On the other hand, the grant (at less than the full cost) of a capital interest in the LLC generally would be subject to the expense recognition rules of ASC 718.

As discussed in previous chapters, employees in an LLC frequently receive a profits interest in the company rather than a capital interest. This allows the employees to share in the profits of the business and receive a cash payment (either annually or on a deferred basis) rather than gain an ownership interest in the company that may increase in value over time. As discussed further below, the accounting for a profits interest generally is different from that for a capital interest.

Measurement

The first step in determining the accounting for an LLC interest is to measure the total amount of that expense. This may differ among the various types of LLC ownership interests, which are discussed in chapters 2 and 3 of this book.

Capital Interest

A capital interest in an LLC is similar to restricted stock in a corporation. In both cases the employee has an ownership interest in the capital or equity of the organization. Consequently, the accounting for both is similar. The employer must recognize an expense for the fair value of the capital interest that the employee is receiving for services rendered. In the case of a publicly traded company, the fair value generally is equal to the traded value of the stock or unit as determined by the public markets. Because most LLCs are privately held, however, determining fair value is more difficult. One indicator of fair value would be a reference to a recent similar transaction for a capital interest that was purchased by an unrelated third party. In the absence of such a purchase, it may be necessary to obtain an appraisal or other determination of value from an independent professional. In some cases, it may be helpful to establish a formula value that would be used for purposes of buying and selling capital interests in the LLC.

In 2011 the American Institute of Certified Public Accountants (AICPA) revised its Practice Aid to guide privately held companies with the valuation of their equity securities issued for purposes of employee compensation. The AICPA Practice Aid indicates that the valuation of these equity securities should be conducted using any of three acceptable valuation methods:

- Market
- Income (e.g., discounted cash flows)
- Asset

Although independent appraisers have used other commonly accepted valuation methods, only these three meet the guidelines established in the Practice Aid. Also, although all of the methodologies detailed in the Practice Aid are used by valuation specialists, the Practice Aid indicates a preference for different methods based on various characteristics or other criteria specific to each company's circumstances.

Furthermore, the Practice Aid provides a hierarchy of valuation methodologies to indicate a preference for the type of valuation private companies should use. Preferably, the valuation should be conducted by an unrelated valuation specialist contemporaneously with the issuance of the compensatory equity. If that is not possible, the next preferred approach is a retrospective valuation by an unrelated valuation specialist. The least preferred method for valuing the securities is a valuation established by a "related party valuation specialist."

Valuations that are performed consistent with the guidelines detailed in the AICPA Practice Aid will be more likely to meet the approval of the company's auditors. With respect to private companies that undergo an initial public offering (IPO), the SEC has accepted valuations of employee equity using the AICPA Practice Aid and has not challenged these valuations. This is a significant departure from the SEC's previous practice of challenging the valuation of employee equity issued in the year prior to an IPO under its "cheap stock" theory. This often resulted in companies recognizing an additional compensation expense at the time of the IPO in order to gain SEC approval. Instead, companies following the guidelines of the AICPA Practice Aid for the valuation of employee equity generally will not be challenged by the SEC in this regard.

Option to Purchase Capital Interest

The grant of an option to purchase a capital interest in the LLC will be treated similarly to a stock option, which allows an employee to buy corporate stock at a time of his or her choosing within a specified time frame and at agreed-upon terms. Unlike previous accounting rules of APB 25, ASC 718 requires the use of special valuation models for determining the value of the option. The LLC may choose to use a closed-form valuation model (e.g., Black-Scholes) or an open-form approach such as the binomial model. The FASB has no preference which formula the employer chooses, provided that it is applied consistently. Most companies use the Black-Scholes formulation because of its simplicity. Both approaches require the use of six valuation assumptions:

- Fair value of the underlying equity (e.g., capital interest)
- Exercise price of the option
- Life or term of the option
- Prevailing risk-free interest rate
- Volatility of the price of the underlying capital interest
- Dividend yields of the capital interest, if any

Each of these assumptions must be calculated or estimated by the company. Under the Black-Scholes approach, each of the valuation factors is assumed to remain constant throughout the life of the option. In contrast, the open-form model allows the employer to assume that the valuation assumptions will change over the life of the option as well as to consider other factors (e.g., the probability of employee turnover) that may affect the value of the option.

Each of the valuation assumptions is determined for an LLC similar to the way it would be for a corporation. The most difficult one, however, is the determination of volatility. Assuming the LLC is a privately held company, it is difficult or impractical to measure the expected volatility of an LLC unit. Instead, the LLC is required to measure its options to purchase a capital interest based on a value determined by using the historical volatility of an appropriate industry sector index instead of the expected volatility of an LLC unit price.

Profits Interest

Unlike the capital interest in an LLC, a profits interest provides only for a share of future net income of the LLC. Although the terms of the profits interest may allow the employee to sell his or her interest in the LLC, it does not represent any ownership of the underlying capital or equity of the company. It is merely a right to a future cash payment based on company profits. ASC 718 addresses situations in which employee awards are settled in cash rather than an ownership interest in the business. It specifically provides for "liability" accounting in such cases.

The accounting rules allow the private company to make a "policy decision" about how to account for liability awards. The company may use either fair value or intrinsic value for award valuation purposes.

Regardless of which approach is used, the profits interest is valued at the grant date (similar to the treatment of capital interests). Furthermore, in each subsequent accounting period the profits interest is subject to mark-to-market treatment until the award is settled. The result is that the company recognizes an expense for all cash payments made to the employee while the employee holds the profits interest rather than fixing the expense at the initial date of grant.

Carried Interest

As noted in chapter 2, another form of compensation that is common to many LLCs (particularly private equity and hedge funds) is the "carried interest," a perceived form of equity. A carried interest provides the employee with the right to share in the profits of the LLC, similar to a profits interest. In some cases a carried interest is nothing more than a bonus arrangement, whereas in others it may entitle the employee to a predetermined portion of the LLC profits, calculated after all expenses have been paid. Although the carried interest is not actually equity in the LLC, it can be designed in a manner that provides the holder with an ongoing right to future income and that can be sold or otherwise transferred to others, depending on its terms and the LLC's operating agreement.

LLC Equity Appreciation Rights

As discussed above, phantom LLC units track periodic profits distributed by the LLC, similar to stock appreciation rights in a corporation. The employee receives no LLC ownership interest other than the right to receive periodic cash payments. Consequently, LLC equity appreciation rights will be accounted for in the same manner as profits interests using liability accounting.

Compensation Expense Accruals

Once the amount of compensation expense has been determined under equity accounting, the aggregate expense must be amortized over the employee's service period. This is usually the same as the vesting period. If the vesting occurs all at the end of the service period, the total expense is amortized on a level (straight-line) basis so that the same amount of expense is recognized each year during the service period.

If the employee gradually vests each year during the service period, the employer may choose either straight-line or multiple-option amortization. By using the multiple-option approach, the amount of the expense to be recognized each year is treated as a separate award and amortized accordingly. For example an award that vests ratably over three years is treated as a grant of three separate awards: an award vesting in one year, an award vesting in two years, and an award vesting in three years. Each year's award is expensed over its appropriate vesting period. The net result is an expense in the first year consisting of 100% of the first year's award, plus 50% of the second year's award, plus 33% of the third year's award. The second year expense is equal to 50% of the second year's award plus 33% of the third year's award. The third year expense would consist of only the remaining portion of the third year's award (i.e., 33%). Because of the front-loading effect of multiple-option amortization as well as its complexity, most companies use straight-line amortization.

Vesting Conditions

The basis for determining an employee's vesting in the award may affect the amount of expense recognized for that award. If the vesting is based on service or performance conditions, no compensation expense is recognized for awards that are forfeited as a result of termination of employment or performance conditions not achieved. Forfeitures are estimated at the time of grant, and the estimate is eventually trued up based on actual experience during the vesting period. Additionally, compensation expense attributable to forfeited awards that was recognized in prior periods is reversed in the period of forfeiture.

If vesting is somehow tied to the value of the LLC (e.g., attainment of a predetermined unit value), no adjustments are made for forfeitures. Because the typical LLC is not publicly traded, this provision is seldom seen in LLC awards.

Income Tax Benefit

Generally, most LLCs in the U.S. choose to be taxed as partnerships rather than as corporations. As such, those LLCs do not benefit from any tax deductions associated with equity compensation. Instead, the LLC's owners (i.e., the unit holders) benefit from the tax deduction because of the pass-through nature of partnership income.

If the nature of an award is expected to produce a tax deduction for the LLC, however, the benefit of that tax deduction must be taken into account in determining the net cost of the equity award. Because of the differences in the timing of an expense of an award (at grant) and the tax deduction for that award (vesting, exercise, or payout), determining the relevant amounts of the future tax deductions is more complicated. The tax benefit is calculated based on the grant date value of the equity award and the company's effective tax rate.

The LLC must maintain a pool of unused tax benefits that would have been recognized under FAS 123 between 1995 and 2005. Furthermore, any additional tax benefits that arise after 2005 and are not included in income (see next paragraph) are added to the pool.

If the ultimate tax benefit is greater than the expected tax benefit, the surplus is credited to capital in the balance sheet. Also, it is included in the pool of unused tax benefits (see previous paragraph). It does not flow through the income statement and thus is not included in net income or earnings per share. If the actual tax benefit is less than the expected tax benefit, the shortfall reduces the pool of unused tax benefits and need not be taken into account as an expense. If things reach a point where no surplus tax benefits remain in the pool, the remaining shortfall is charged to earnings as additional income tax expense.

Modifications

In the event that an award is subsequently modified, it is treated as the exchange of the original award for a new equity award. A modification is deemed to occur when there is a change in any of the award's terms or conditions. An additional compensation expense must be recognized for any incremental fair value of the new award over the fair value of the canceled award. Additionally, any remaining unrecognized compensation cost from the date of grant must also be recognized. Unlike the case with previous accounting rules, determinations of change in value must be measured in terms of fair value rather than intrinsic value. The measurement of additional compensation expense is based on the fair value of the equity award immediately before the modification and immediately after the modification. In no event may the total compensation expense be less than the fair value at the date of grant. Some examples of modifications are:

- Exchanges of equity awards relating to a business combination or in equity restructuring

- Inducements to terminate employment or retire early

- Cash-out of all award values, to the extent payment exceeds the fair value of the award immediately before the cash-out

- Repricing of an equity instrument

Chapter 5

A Primer on Sharing Equity with Employees in Non-LLC Companies

Corey Rosen

This book focuses on equity compensation plans for limited liability companies, but it is important to understand equity compensation in the context of C or S corporations as well for two reasons. First, if you do a Web search for equity compensation plans in LLCs, most of the articles will say that it is a lot easier and often recommended to switch to S or C status instead because the rules and alternative approaches are simpler and more certain. Second, the concepts of sharing equity in an LLC generally parallel concepts in an S or C corporation. By understanding these more familiar concepts, it may be easier to see how their equivalents in LLCs work.

For most LLCs that decide to convert, an S corporation is the logical choice. The tax treatment of S corporations and LLCs is similar in many ways. Both are pass-through entities, meaning there is no corporate level tax. Instead, individual owners pay taxes on any profits and gains. While there are a number of differences, the key difference is that in an S corporation, distributions must be proportional to ownership, whereas an LLC can make distributions in other ways if it so chooses.

The first part of this chapter looks at individual equity plans; these plans can be used for selective or broad-based plans. The second part looks at plans that are designed to benefit most or all employees. This chapter focuses on plan design and tax issues. Securities law considerations are briefly discussed in a separate section, but because this is such a complex subject, they are not reviewed in any detail. Accounting issues are extremely complex and varied for different plans and are discussed only briefly here. For more information on accounting concerns, see the NCEO's books *Accounting for Equity-Based Compensation* (for individual equity plans and employee stock purchase plans) or *Leveraged ESOPs and Employee Buyouts* (for ESOPs).

Basic Forms of Individual Equity Plans

There are four basic kinds of individual equity compensation plans: stock options, restricted stock and restricted stock units, stock appreciation rights, and phantom stock. Many of these plans have variations as well. Each plan provides employees with some special consideration in price or terms. (This chapter does not cover simply offering employees the right to buy stock on the same terms any other investor would receive, or making unrestricted grants of shares.)

Stock options give employees the right to buy a number of shares at a price fixed at grant for a defined number of years into the future. *Restricted stock* (and its close relative *restricted stock units*) give employees the right to acquire or receive shares, by gift or purchase, once certain restrictions, such as working a certain number of years or meeting a performance target, are met. *Phantom stock* pays a future cash bonus equal to the value of a certain number of shares. *Stock appreciation rights* provide the right to the increase in the value of a designated number of shares, usually paid in cash, but occasionally settled in shares (this is called a "stock-settled SAR").

Stock Options

A few key concepts help define how stock options work:

- *Exercise:* The purchase of stock with an option.
- *Exercise price:* The price at which the stock can be purchased. This is also called the *strike price*. In most plans, the exercise price is the current fair market value of the stock at the time the exercise is made.
- *Grant price:* How much the option holder must pay to exercise the option.

- *Spread:* The difference between the grant price and exercise price at the time of exercise.

- *Option term:* The amount of time the employee can hold the option before it expires.

- *Vesting:* The requirement, usually in years of service, that must be met for an option holder to be able to exercise an option.

A company grants an employee options to buy a stated number of shares at a defined grant price. The options vest over a period of time or once certain individual, group, or corporate goals are met. Once vested, the employee can exercise the option at the grant price at any time over the option term up to the expiration date. For instance, an employee might be granted the right to buy 1,000 shares at $10 per share. The options vest 25% per year over four years and have a term of 10 years. If the stock goes up, the employee will pay $10 per share to buy the stock. The difference between the $10 grant price and the exercise price is the spread. If the stock goes to $25 after seven years, and the employee exercises all options, the spread would be $15 per share.

Kinds of Options

Employee stock options are either incentive stock options (ISOs) or nonqualified options (NSOs). When an employee exercises a nonqualified stock option, the spread on exercise is taxable to the employee as ordinary income, even if the shares are not yet sold. A corresponding amount is deductible by the company. There is no legally required holding period for the shares after exercise, although the company may impose one. Any subsequent gain or loss on the shares after exercise is taxed as capital gains or losses.

An incentive stock option (ISO) enables an employee to (1) defer taxation on the option from the date of exercise until the date of sale of the underlying shares and (2) to pay tax at capital gains rates, rather than ordinary income tax rates, on the spread at exercise. Certain conditions must be met to qualify for ISO treatment:

1. The employee must hold the stock for at least one year after the exercise date or two years after the grant date, whichever is later.

2. Only $100,000 of stock options can become exercisable in any year. This is measured by the grant price of the options, not the exercise price. It means that only $100,000 in grant price value can vest (first become exercisable) in any one year. If there is overlapping vesting, such as would occur if options are granted annually and vest gradually, companies must track outstanding options to see if the amount that becomes vested under different grants would exceed $100,000 in grant value in any one year. Any amount exceeding $100,000 is treated as coming from an NSO.

3. The exercise price must be equal to at least 100% of the market price of the company's stock on the date of the grant.

4. Only employees can qualify for an ISO.

5. The option must be granted pursuant to a written plan that has been approved by shareholders, that specifies how many shares can be issued under the plan, and that identifies the class of employees eligible to receive the options. Options must be granted within 10 years of the date of the adoption of the plan.

6. The option cannot by its terms be exercisable more than 10 years after the date of the grant.

7. The employee cannot own, at the time of the grant, more than 10% of the voting power of all outstanding stock of the company, unless the exercise price is at least 110% of the market value of the stock on the date of the grant, and the option is not exercisable more than five years from the date of the grant.

If all the rules for incentive options are met at the time of exercise, then the transaction is called a "qualifying disposition," and the employee pays capital gains tax on the total increase in value at sale over the grant price. However, the spread on the option at exercise is a "preference item" for purposes of the alternative minimum tax (AMT). So even though the shares may not have been sold, the exercise requires the employee to add back the gain on exercise, along with other AMT preference items, to see if an alternative minimum tax payment is due.

The company does not take a tax deduction when there is a qualifying disposition. If, however, there is a disqualifying disposition, most often because the employee exercises and sells before meeting the required holding periods, the spread on exercise is taxable to the employee at ordinary income tax rates, and any capital appreciation on the ISO shares in excess of the market price on exercise of an ISO is taxed at capital gains rates. In this instance, the company may then deduct the spread on exercise.

Exercising an Option

There are four ways to exercise a stock option: cash, the exchange of existing shares (often called a stock swap), same-day sales, and their close relative, sell-to-cover sales (these latter two are often called cashless exercises, although that term actually includes other kinds of exercise methods described here as well). Any one company, however, may provide for just one or two of these alternatives. Private companies do not offer same-day or sell-to-cover sales, and they often restrict the exercise or sale of the shares acquired through exercise until the company is sold or goes public.

The most common form of exercise for an option in a closely held company is simply for the employee to pay cash for the shares. The employee might then have additional taxes due, depending on the kind of option. If the options are nonqualified, the employer might then have to withhold taxes on the spread from the employee's future paychecks, unless the employer can arrange to use some of the option shares to pay for this obligation, as would normally be the case in the kind of cashless transactions described below.

In a same-day sale, the employee works with a broker, usually one provided by the company. The company provides the broker with enough shares to cover the option exercise, the broker turns around and sells them, and the proceeds, minus the exercise price and any taxes due, go to the employee. Although called a "same-day" sale, the process can take up to three days. In a sell-to-cover exercise, the same approach is used, but the broker sells only enough shares to cover the exercise price and any taxes due, giving the employee the remaining value in shares.

In a stock swap, the employee simply exchanges existing shares for the option shares. For instance, if the employee has the right to buy

1,000 shares at $10 per share and the shares are now worth $25, the employee would exchange 400 shares the employee currently owns for the 1,000 shares. That's because the 400 shares the employee owns are worth $10,000. The employee would then get 600 shares from the option. If there are taxes due as well, then the employee might choose to turn in enough shares to cover the taxes as well, although this is not a common strategy. Stock swaps are more commonly used with incentive stock options where taxes do not have to be paid until the newly acquired shares are sold.

Accounting

Under rules for equity compensation plans that became effective in 2006, companies must calculate the present value of all option awards as of the date of grant and show this as a charge to compensation. The value should be adjusted based on vesting experience (so unvested shares do not count as a charge to compensation).

Restricted Stock

Restricted stock provides the employee with the right to purchase shares at fair market value or a discount, or simply grants shares to employees outright. However, the shares employees acquire are not really theirs yet—they cannot take possession of the shares until specified restrictions lapse. Most commonly, the restriction is that the employee works for the company for a certain number of years, often three to five. The time-based restrictions may pass all at once or gradually. Any restrictions could be imposed, however. The company could, for instance, restrict the shares until certain corporate, departmental, or individual performance goals are achieved. With restricted stock units (RSUs), employees do not actually buy or receive shares *until* the restrictions lapse. In effect, RSUs are like phantom stock settled in shares instead of cash.

While the shares are subject to restrictions, companies can choose whether to pay dividends, provide voting rights, or give the employee other benefits of being a shareholder. When employees are awarded the restricted stock, they have the right to make what is called a "Section 83(b)" election. If they make the election, they are taxed at ordinary income tax rates on the "bargain element" of the award at the time of grant. If the shares are simply granted to the employee, then the bargain element is their full value. If some consideration is paid, then the tax is based on the difference between what is paid and the fair market value at the time of the grant. If full price is paid, there is no tax. Any future increase in the value of the shares until they are sold is then taxed as capital gains, not ordinary income. If employees do not make the election, then there is no tax until the restrictions lapse, at which time ordinary income tax is due on the difference between the grant and exercise price. Subsequent changes in value are capital gains (or losses). Employees cannot make the Section 83(b) election for RSUs.

The employer gets a tax deduction only for amounts employees pay income tax on, regardless of whether a Section 83(b) election is made or not. A Section 83(b) election carries some risk. If the employee makes the election and pays tax, but the restrictions never lapse, the employee does not get the taxes paid refunded, nor does the employee get the shares.

Restricted stock accounting parallels option accounting in most respects. If the only restriction is vesting, companies account for restricted stock by first determining the total compensation cost at the time the award is made. So if the employee is simply given 1,000 restricted shares worth $10 per share, then a $10,000 cost is incurred. If the employee buys the shares at fair value, no charge is recorded; if there is a discount, that counts as a cost. The cost is then amortized over the period of vesting until the restrictions lapse. Because the accounting is based on the initial cost, companies with a low share price will find that a vesting requirement for the award means their accounting charge will be very low even if the stock price goes up.

If the award is more contingent, such as performance vesting, the value must be adjusted each year for the current stock price, then amortized over the estimated life of the award (the time estimated to meet the performance goal). Each year, the expected cost is amortized over the estimated remaining expected life. So if the stock is awarded at $10 and goes to $15 in the first year of an expected five-year term, then $15 x 1,000 x . 20 is recorded ($3,000). If the price goes to $18 the next year, the calculation is $18 x 1,000 x .40 ($3,600). The prior $2,000 is subtracted from this amount, yielding a charge of $1,800 for that year.

Phantom Stock and Stock Appreciation Rights

Stock appreciation rights (SARs) and phantom stock are very similar plans. Both essentially are cash bonus plans, although some plans pay out the benefits in the form of shares. SARs typically provide the employee with a cash payment based on the increase in the value of a stated number of shares over a specific period of time. Phantom stock provides a cash or stock bonus based on the value of a stated number of shares, to be paid out at the end of a specified period of time. SARs may not have a specific settlement date; like options, the employees may have flexibility in when to choose to exercise the SAR. Phantom stock may pay dividends; SARs generally do not. When the payout is made, it is taxed as ordinary income to the employee and is deductible to the employer. Some phantom plans condition the receipt of the award on meeting certain objectives, such as sales, profits, or other targets. These plans often call their phantom stock "performance units."

Because SARs and phantom plans are essentially cash bonuses or are delivered in the form of stock that holders will want to cash in, companies need to figure out how to pay for them. Does the company just make a promise to pay or does it really put aside the funds? If the award is paid in stock, is there a market for the stock? If it is only a promise, will employees believe the benefit is as phantom as the stock? If it is in real funds set aside for this purpose, the company will be putting after-tax dollars aside instead of using them in the business. Many small, growth-oriented companies cannot afford to do this. The fund can also be subject to excess accumulated earnings tax. On the other hand, if employees are given shares, the shares can be paid for by capital markets if the company goes public or by acquirers if the company is sold.

If phantom stock or SARs are irrevocably promised to employees, it is possible the benefit will become taxable before employees actually receive the funds. A "rabbi trust," a segregated account to fund deferred payments to employees, may help solve the accumulated earnings problem, but if the company is unable to pay creditors with existing funds, the money in these trusts goes to them. Telling employees their right to the benefit is not irrevocable, or is dependent on some condition (working another five years, for instance), may prevent the money from being currently taxable, but it may also weaken employee belief that the benefit is real.

Finally, if phantom stock or SARs are intended to benefit most or all employees and defer some or all payment until termination or later, they may be considered a de facto "ERISA plan." ERISA (the Employee Retirement Income Security Act of 1974) is the federal law that governs retirement plans. It does not allow non-ERISA plans to operate like ERISA plans, so the plan could be ruled subject to all the constraints of ERISA. Similarly, if there is an explicit or implied reduction in compensation to get the phantom stock, there could be securities issues involved, most likely anti-fraud disclosure requirements. Plans designed just for a limited number of employees, or as a bonus for a broader group of employees that pays out annually based on a measure of equity, would most likely avoid these problems. Moreover, the regulatory issues are "gray areas"; it could be that a company could use a broad-based plan that pays over longer periods or at departure and not ever be challenged.

Phantom stock and SAR accounting is straightforward. These plans are treated in the same way as deferred cash compensation. As the amount of the liability changes each year, an entry is made for the amount accrued. A decline in value would create a negative entry. These entries are not contingent on vesting. In closely held companies, share value is often stated as book value. However, this can dramatically underrate the true value of a company, especially one based primarily on intellectual capital. Having an outside appraisal performed, therefore, can make the plans much more accurate rewards for employee contributions.

Employee Stock Purchase Plans

Millions of employees become owners in their companies through employee stock purchase plans (ESPPs). Many of these plans are organized under Section 423 of the tax code and thus are often called "Section 423" plans. Other ESPPs are "nonqualified" plans, meaning they do not have to meet the special rules of Section 423 and do not get any of the special tax treatment.

Under Section 423, companies must allow all employees to participate but can exclude those with less than two years' tenure, part-time employees, and highly compensated employees. All employees must have the same rights and privileges under the plan, although companies can allow purchase limits to vary with relative compensation (most do not do this, however). Plans can limit how much employees can buy, and the law limits it to $25,000 per year.

Section 423 plans operate by allowing employees to have deductions taken out of their pay on an after-tax basis. These deductions accumulate over an "offering period." At a specified time or times employees can choose to use these accumulated deductions to purchase shares, or they can get the money back. Plans can offer discounts of up to 15% on the price of the stock. Most plans allow this discount to be taken based on *either* the price at the beginning or end of the offering period (the so-called "look-back feature"). The offering period can last up to five years if the price employees pay for their stock is based on the share price at the end of the period or 27 months if it can be determined at an earlier point.

Plan design can vary in a number of ways. For instance, a company might allow employees a 15% discount on the price at the end of the offering period, but no discount if they buy shares based on the price at the beginning of the period. Some companies offer employees interim opportunities to buy shares during the offering period. Others provide smaller discounts. Offering periods also vary in length. NCEO studies, however, show that the large majority of plans have a look-back feature and provide 15% discounts off the share price at the beginning or end of the offering period. Most of the plans have a 12-month offering period, with six months the next most common.

The tax treatment of a Section 423 plan is similar to that of an incentive stock option plan. If employees hold the shares for two years after grant and one year after exercise, they pay ordinary income tax on the lesser of (1) the discount element as of the beginning of the offering period and (2) the amount by which the sale price exceeds the purchase price. Any additional gain is taxed as a long-term capital gain. The company gets no tax deduction, even on the discount. There is no withholding requirement on the gain on the employee purchase of shares.

If these rules are not met, employees pay ordinary income tax on the difference between the exercise price and the fair market value of the stock on the purchase date, plus long-term or short-term capital gains taxes on any increase in value over the purchase price. The company gets a tax deduction for the spread between the purchase price and the exercise price.

Nonqualified ESPPs usually work much the same way, but there are no rules for how they must be structured and no special tax benefits. The employee would pay tax on the discount as ordinary income *at the time the stock is purchased* and would pay capital gains on any subsequent gain.

ESPPs are found almost exclusively in public companies because the offering of stock to employees requires compliance with costly and complex securities laws. Closely held companies can, and sometimes do, have these plans, however. Offerings of stock only to employees can qualify for an exemption from securities registration requirements at the federal level, although they will have to comply with anti-fraud disclosure rules and, possibly, state securities laws as well. If they do offer stock in a stock purchase plan, it is highly advisable to obtain at least an annual appraisal.

ESPPs are very popular in public companies and some pre-IPO companies (where the plan starts before the IPO, and purchases are not made until after it) as they offer a benefit to employees and additional capital to companies. Any dilution resulting from the issuance of new shares to satisfy the purchase requests, or from the company repurchasing outstanding shares and reselling them at a discount, is usually so small that shareholders do not object. Rates of participation vary widely, with the median levels around 30% to 40% of eligible employees. Because most employees do not commit large amounts to these plans, and many do not participate at all, ESPPs should generally be seen as an adjunct to other employee ownership plans, not a means in themselves to create an ownership culture.

ESPPs are accounted for in the same way as options. Any discount offered counts as a compensation charge, and the present value of the option element must be calculated as an additional charge to income.

Securities Law Issues

If employees are given a right to purchase shares, the offer is subject to securities laws. The two key elements of securities laws are registration and disclosure. Registration means the filing of documents with the state and/or federal securities agencies concerning the employer whose stock is being sold. There are registration procedures for small offerings of stock (under $1 million or $5 million, depending on the procedure) that can be done for relatively small legal fees (as little as $10,000 in some cases), but larger offerings require a lot of complex paperwork, and fees often exceed $100,000. Registration requires the filing of audited financial statements and continuing reporting obligations to the federal Securities and Exchange Commission (SEC) and appropriate state agencies.

Disclosure refers to providing information to buyers about what they are getting, similar to, but frequently less detailed than, what would be in a prospectus. At times, there are specific state and federal rules about what needs to go in these documents, including objective discussions of risks, the financial condition of the firm, officers' and directors' salaries, and other information. In the absence of requirements for the registration of the securities, disclosure is intended to satisfy the anti-fraud requirements of federal and state laws.

Generally, offers to sell securities (stocks, bonds, etc.) require registration of those securities unless there is a specific exemption. In addition, companies with 500 or more shareholders and more than $10 million in assets are considered public firms under federal law and must comply with the reporting requirements of the Exchange Act of 1934 even if they do not have to register under the Securities Act of 1933. (An exemption added by the SEC in 2007 allows companies to exclude holders of unexercised compensatory employee stock options from the 500-shareholder calculation if the company otherwise does not have to report under the Exchange Act.)

There are a number of exemptions from these rules listed below. These are exemptions from registration; any time stock is offered, it should include appropriate financial disclosure to satisfy anti-fraud rules.

The most important of these exemptions is Rule 701. Under federal law, offers to a company's employees, directors, general partners, trustees, officers, or certain consultants (those providing services to a company similar to what an employer might hire someone to do, but not consultants who help raise capital) can be made under a written compensation agreement. If total sales during a 12-month period do not exceed the greater of: $1 million, 15% of the issuer's total assets, or 15% of all the outstanding securities of that class, then the offerings are exempt from registration requirements. The offerings must be discrete (not included in any other offer) and are still subject to disclosure requirements. For total sales under $5 million during a 12-month period to the specified class of people above, companies must comply with anti-fraud disclosure rules; for sales of over this amount, companies must disclose additional information, including risk factors, copies of the plans under which the offerings are made, and certain financial statements. These disclosures must be made to all shareholders.

For purposes of this rule, options are considered part of the aggregate sales price, with the option price defined as of the date of grant. In calculating outstanding securities for the 15% rule, all currently exercisable or convertible options, warrants, restricted stock, stock rights, and other securities are counted.

Other exemptions are available for sale to a limited number of accredited or sophisticated investors with appropriate information (these terms are legally defined and generally include officers, directors and/or higher income individuals); small offerings to 35 or fewer non-accredited investors; offerings under $500,000; and offerings only to in-state residents if the offeror does 80% or more of its business and has 80% or more of its assets in-state.

These exemptions from registration are available under federal law. Some states track federal exemptions; some do not. Thirty-nine states have "blue sky laws" (the general name for state securities laws) that comply with the Uniform Securities Act, which is partly based on federal law. Perhaps most important for offerings to employees, however, states that have a specific exemption parallel to the federal Rule 701 exemption (for offerings to employees) are the exception rather than the rule. State registration for such offerings may be needed, therefore, unless other exemptions are met.

Public companies cannot use Rule 701 for an exemption from securities law filings. Instead, most rely on Form S-8, a simplified registration form that can be used to comply with securities laws in conjunction with an offering of options. Public companies do not have to offer a formal prospectus to potential buyers, as closely held companies would. They are, however, required to provide information to employee stock purchasers about the company and its option plan. The S-8 form allows that to be done by reference to already available public documents.

Public companies must also make sure their plan design complies with trading restrictions that apply to corporate insiders. This requires the filing of various reports and the restriction of some trading activity, among other things. These issues are too technical for adequate discussion here. Public companies should consult with their legal counsel on these matters before designing their plan.

Chapter 6

Communicating with Employees About Equity

Corey Rosen

Companies usually create equity plans, at least in part, to attract, retain, and motivate employees. That makes sense. Companies that employ good people and have strong corporate cultures of employee engagement have a huge competitive edge. They are also in a buyer's market for employees, who will look on the company's culture with particular favor. Even in difficult times, companies that can maintain employee engagement are much more likely to survive, in part because engaged employees are more likely to come up with innovative ideas for saving money and generating new products.

One of the most important ways companies can maintain or build cultures of engagement is by linking their equity programs to a broader corporate culture that treats people like owners. Plan design matters as well—who gets equity, how much they get, when they get it, what triggers an award, and when it becomes liquid all can reinforce a shared sense of ownership or undermine it. An effective equity plan cannot simply be a potentially very lucrative carrot dangled in front of employees in the hopes they will make extraordinary efforts to help the company succeed. While a few exceptional companies do become the Googles and Microsofts that create legendary numbers of very wealthy employees, the usual story is far more modest, with equity being a welcome and even substantial added benefit, but nonetheless just one part of a three-legged stool of base pay, benefits, and equity that make up a good compensation package.

The research on employee ownership, employee turnover, corporate performance, and employee engagement is very consistent. Studies since the 1980s through a recent analysis published by the National Bureau of Economic Research of what is probably the largest data set ever compiled on employee attitudes, organizational culture, and organizational performance show that for shared ownership plans to work, they must both be communicated effectively and be linked to high-engagement management styles.[1] These include sharing corporate performance data, work teams, ad hoc committees, devolving decision-making to the lowest possible level, and other ways to help employees share ideas and information.

Effective communication helps people understand what they are getting, when they will get it, and what they need to do, individually and as members of the organization, to earn it. People will come away knowing the realistic benefits and rewards of equity in your company's specific environment, not in an imagined environment of stories they have heard about equity riches (or losses) in highly publicized (and thus by definition atypical) cases. High-involvement management allows employees to use the motivation the equity can provide not just to make more effort but to generate the ideas that can move companies forward in far more substantial ways than extra effort ever can.

This chapter provides guidance on how to communicate equity sharing specifically in an LLC as well as strategies to get people more involved.

Explaining How Your Equity Plan Works

Helping employees understand how their equity plans work is not an easy task. Most employees have only a vague and often inaccurate idea

---

1. Douglas L. Kruse, Joseph R. Blasi, and Richard B. Freeman, "Does Linking Worker Pay to Firm Performance Help the Best Firms Do Even Better?," NBER Working Paper No. 17745 (January 2012) (see http://www.nber.org/papers/w17745). The research was done in 2011 and looked at over 300,000 survey respondents in 730 companies that had applied for the "100 Best Companies to Work For in America" list. The list is the creation of the Great Place to Work Institute. The data also include extensive information about company structures and practices.

of how companies make money, what percentage of sales are profits, how stock prices are determined by the market or an appraiser, and how shares get created. Equity awards add another layer of complexity onto that because they are rarely just outright grants of shares but come layered with special rules, and equity awards in particular can add yet another layer of complexity because few people understand how an LLC works.

To create a good communications plan, it is important first to understand what makes any kind of communication effective. Several key strategies are critical:

• As many people have reputedly said, it is not what people know that hurts them, it is what they know that just ain't so. It is essential that companies use surveys and/or focus groups to find out what people know "that just ain't so" so that they can address these issues.

• Divide the communications program into lots of smaller bites delivered regularly. One time, you might explain what stock is; another time, what the tax rules for the awards are. It is easier for people to absorb smaller amounts of information, and the regular provision of communications about the equity awards in itself is a powerful communication that these awards matter.

• Use multiple media—a FAQ on your Web site, printed materials sent to employee homes, videos, interactive tools to model how an equity award would gain value under various realistic assumptions, small-group meetings, annual all-hands meetings, etc.

• As much as possible, use other employees to explain the plans, not experts. Experts have a hard time remembering what they did not once know and hence assume people understand ideas they do not. Peers don't have that problem and are more credible to other employees as well. To be sure, what they do needs to be vetted by experts, but companies that use peer-based communications find it works very well.

• Provide concrete, specific examples, not just general concepts.

• Don't oversell the plan. Our research shows that employees much prefer honest explanations of potential risks as well as rewards—it shows you are willing to treat them as adults, indeed as fellow owners.

• Use stories. The more that your communication can be based on stories of how the awards have worked for other employees (even if they are in other companies), the more resonant they are. There is a reason newspaper stories on complex topics always start with a story of a specific family or situation—it works.

Given these general principles, you also have to explain plan specifics. People want to know what they will get, when they will get it, what the rules are, and how much they will pay. Use examples to illustrate each point, with scenarios of both rising and falling prices. By focusing just on these issues, doing it often in small bites, and using multiple approaches to explain the same thing, chances are good most employees will get a clear understanding over time. Sadly, however, few companies do much of any of this—they send out a form, a letter from the CEO, and a plan summary, and consider it done. The result is that they spend lots of money on the awards and have lots of confused, uninterested employees.

In an LLC, good communication has to start with explaining how the LLC works. Many people do not know how corporate profits are taxed in general, but, to the extent they do, their model is a C corporation. So companies need to start by explaining that in an LLC, the taxes are passed through to the owners and the board can decide how to allocate the tax obligation (or, if it is done pro-rata in your company, just say that). If your company provides employees with capital interests or profits interests, in general, if they have made a Section 83(b) election and become fully vested, they are treated as a member of the LLC and issued a K-1 statement. This can be an unpleasant and confusing surprise, so make sure that (1) employees fully understand the implications of an 83(b) election and (2) what happens if they get a K-1 statement. Will they receive a distribution of earnings to pay the tax, or is it their responsibility? If the awards are LLC units or unit appreciation rights, this is not an issue.

Second, you need to be very clear about both how awards are issued and why. Lots of companies do the first, but most gloss over the second, just saying it is to reward people. Be very clear about why employees get what they get, what they have to do to earn it, and what you expect from them in return. Perhaps most important, lay out precisely when they will get cashed in. Is it at a sale or IPO only? If so, why? What if employees leave before an event occurs? What if it is uncertain when, or even if it will occur? If there is interim liquidity, explain that too. Again, explain in clear, honest terms why you are making these choices.

Finally, explain how they get other questions answered, the procedures for acknowledging the grant, noncompete agreements (if any), when they will get statements, and any other procedural matters. Do not assume people will ask about these or any other issues. Certainly you want to have a Q&A, but often people feel reluctant or embarrassed to ask a question, especially the first one. Instead, try asking people to write down a question before coming to a meeting and then posting FAQs on your internal Web site.

Sharing Your Numbers Honestly

No matter what decisions your company makes about its equity program design and operation, it is essential to have open and honest communications about how your company is doing. The defining characteristic of the Great Place to Work Institute's "100 Best Companies to Work For in America" is what Robert Levering and Amy Lyman call the "trust index." It measures just how much employees trust management and how much they trust management to trust them.

One of the best ways to build trust is open-book management. Companies using open-book management make a regular practice of keeping employees informed about how the company is doing. Employees feel a lot more like owners when this information is shared. While it is useful to share income statement basics and stock price changes, it is even more useful to share "critical numbers." These are the measures company leaders use to gauge just how they are doing week to week, month to month, and year to year. They are what drives company success, what leaders worry about if they are not being met. Critical numbers at the corporate level may be profits, but they might also be new customers, new patents, customer service, repeat buyers, overhead absorption, sales growth, and so on. At the operational level, each unit of a company also has critical numbers that measure its contribution.

Sharing these numbers helps employees focus on what matters. It is also very motivating. People will happily play slot machines for hours, even though they usually lose, because there is a game attached. But if they were paid, say, $50 for five hours of pushing the buttons, with no rewards for winning or costs for losing, casinos would go out of business. Business is also a game and is much more fun to play if you know the numbers. Jack Stack, the CEO of SRC, the leading thinker about these issues, says that not keeping employees informed about the score in business is like not telling basketball players who is winning.

In entrepreneurial companies that are looking to be sold or do an IPO, it is especially important to discuss the expected timing of that event, what the company needs to do to prepare for it, what milestones need to be met along the way to reach the company's goals, and what employees can specifically do to help reach them. Too often, company leaders occasionally say that their goal is one of these two events, but employees are left in the dark about management's vision of how to reach them.

Imagine that you are an employee who has just received an equity interest in your company. You've been told the goal is to find another buyer one day so that everyone's equity will be worth a substantial sum. But you have no idea when this might occur, what you can do to make the company more attractive to a potential buyer, or what might happen to your job if you are acquired. All that uncertainty will lead you to view the equity award as a far more iffy proposition than it really is. If you do not plan to be sold, then you need to explain what targets the company needs to reach to make it possible to provide interim liquidity (if you have no idea how that will happen, your plan is not really very valuable to anyone).

Your company may also have outside investors. People should know what their roles and expectations are. If there are subsequent investment rounds, explain what this means for the company and the value of the employees' equity interests. As with any other aspect of communicating about equity, you can either explain what is really going on or allow employees to develop their own, usually inaccurate, assumptions.

It is also critical to help employees understand how the company's equity attains value. Very few people understand this process. In most companies, the value of equity is a function of potential future profits.

Investors will pay some multiple of expected future earnings to acquire the company. How much they pay depends on the rate of return they expect, which in turn is driven by what else they could do with the money and how much risk your projected future earnings entail.

One way we at the NCEO explain this to employees is our "Harry the Horse" game. We divide employees into groups of six to eight people. Half are sellers and half are buyers of Harry, a three-year-old racehorse that, after all costs, made $50,000 in profit last year and may be able to race for several more years. The buyers come up with a price they would offer and the sellers a price they would sell for, and then they negotiate. Each group reports back its results (some groups never find common ground) and the factors that led to them. The leader adds other factors that come into play that were not raised. Factors should include Harry-specific risks, industry risks, economy risks, returns on investments of varying risk, how tied up the money will be for how long, and Harry's long-term asset value (stud fees if he races well, glue if not). Then explain that investors look at all these things, estimate the combination of the present value of Harry's future earnings and asset value, and decide, given the risk of buying Harry versus other invest-ments (stocks, bonds, buying stock in one company, etc.) what rate of return they need. If they want a 25% return, then they would pay four times earnings, including stud fees or the going rate of glue.

The point of the game is not to educate people about horse racing, but to show that a potential investor would look at your company in much the same way. The key takeaway is that for each additional dol-lar of profit the company makes, the stock price (or, in this case, the member interest price) increases not by one dollar but by some multiple, such as four in the above example. That helps people understand why ownership can be uniquely valuable if you make profits or can convince investors one day you will.

Note that there are some technology companies where profits matter much less. Their model may be that that if they develop a significant new technology, even one they cannot make money on, another company may buy them because it believes that it can make a profit on it. If that is your business model, then the critical numbers you need to focus on relate to progress toward the development of that product or products.

Creating an Ownership Culture

The common notion is that if employees are granted significant equity stakes in their companies, they will be motivated to think and act like owners. To some extent, this can happen. The image of the 20-something software engineer spending 80-plus hours a week and sleeping on the floor under his desk while working all weekend to get a program out is not just apocryphal. But motivation at work turns out to be a lot more complex than rational calculations about money. The best-selling author Daniel Pink, for instance, says the keys to motivating people at work are purpose, autonomy, and challenge. Financial rewards do matter, he says, if only because absent them people feel manipulated. But when motivation is based solely on money, work can become a chore, not a passion. Moreover, when the reward shrinks or disappears, even for a time, people can become severely demotivated.

As I was writing this, for instance, I saw a story about an employee at Zynga. After it went public, its share price tanked. Some insiders had been able to get out and make vast sums of money, but employees were subject to lock-ups before selling their restricted stock shares and ended up with awards worth little or nothing. One employee was quoted as saying that he worked 100 hours weeks for three years before the IPO in anticipation of a huge payoff even though he felt his managers treated him badly and he didn't really like the job. That story might have been very different if he felt that his work was intrinsically rewarding, that he was treated well by managers, and that his job had a larger purpose. Indeed, companies like Google and Southwest Airlines, both of which use broad-based equity awards, have maintained high employee motivation even during sharp slumps in share prices, because either cultures are so strong and people feel much more like owners in terms of how the company treats them day to day.

So what makes for this kind of ownership culture? The research on this point, including the huge project with the 100 Best Companies to Work For in America list referred to earlier, is very clear. The best companies not only use open-book management but also create specific structures for employees to share ideas and information. These commonly include work teams, ad hoc groups, devolution of decision-making authority to lower-level employees, company-wide staff meetings to discuss ideas and strategy, Web-based systems for collaboration and idea sharing, and other approaches to make employee involvement not just something that is allowed (as in open-door policies) but an expected part of the job.

Conclusion

It doesn't make sense to give away significant equity in your company and then not make a sustained effort to make sure people know how it works, how the company makes money and grows, and how owner-ship interests attain value. But the real communications are not just what you say but what you do. Companies that communicate owner-ship by sharing their performance numbers and creating structured opportunities (and expectations) that employees will contribute ideas and information to move the company forward can—and, the research shows, do—significantly outperform their more conventional peers.

Using the Sample Plan Documents

*This book includes a set of sample documents (on an included CD for the print version of the book, and as part of the zipped file for the digital version). This appendix provides an overview of the documents and their use. **For a list of the specific documents and their filenames, see the end of this appendix.***

A limited liability company (LLC) is not a recognized entity for federal tax purposes and must elect to be treated as a corporation, partnership, or disregarded entity for tax purposes.[1] This means that an LLC may structure its equity incentive plans in a manner similar to the equity incentive structures of traditional C or S corporations (restricted units, options to purchase units, unit appreciation rights, etc.) or of partnerships (profits interests, capital interests, etc.), as applicable, depending on how the LLC has elected to be treated for tax purposes.

Due to the wide variance in incentive structures, it is difficult to prepare a model plan or arrangement that covers every conceivable alternative. Nonetheless, two samples of some common equity incentive structures that an LLC may adopt are included in the form documents included with this book. However, an LLC must ensure that the equity incentive structure(s) that it selects, as with other forms of compensation and benefits (to employees or otherwise), must comply with the applicable provisions of the Internal Revenue Code of 1986, as amended (the "Code"), and the regulations promulgated thereunder, as well as any restrictions under the law of the state in which the LLC is formed.[2]

---

1. "Limited Liability Company (LLC)," available at http://www.irs.gov/businesses/small/article/0,,id=98277,00.html (last updated February 16, 2012).

2. The most recently enacted statute applicable to such incentive arrangements is Section 409A of the Code. 26 U.S.C. § 409A (added under the

This introduction provides a brief outline of the sample documents and their potential uses. It does not substitute for a substantive discussion of all of the considerations needed when implementing an equity incentive plan, and it does not address state law considerations at all. Furthermore, direct grants of profits interests, capital interests, or units in an LLC should accord with the LLC's operating agreement, and they may be subject to additional requirements under the laws of the state in which the LLC is formed. By publishing these sample documents, neither the publisher (the National Center for Employee Ownership [NCEO]) nor the authors or their law firm shall be deemed to be providing legal advice. Before using any of the sample documents, an LLC must consult with its own legal and accounting advisors.

Companies Choosing to Be Taxed as Corporations

While the default alternative for an LLC is to be taxed as a flow-through entity in which the entity pays no taxes and the owners of the LLC pay taxes based on their personal tax rates, a minority of LLCs choose to be taxed as C corporations. This may be because, in the C corporation case, the corporate tax rates are substantially lower than the owners' personal tax rates or the LLC wants to offer certain benefit plans to key employees that are deductible only if the LLC chooses to be taxed as a C corporation. Choosing C corporation status makes it easier to retain large amounts of profits in the entity than being taxed as a pass-through entity because the earnings would be taxable to the owners even if not paid out. C corporations subject owners to double taxation at the corporate and individual level on any profits and/or asset sales. Choosing to be taxed as an S corporation retains the pass-through

American Jobs Creation Act of 2004, Pub. L. No. 108-357, § 885, 118 Stat. 1418 (2004)). In subsequent guidance, the Internal Revenue Service (IRS) noted that deferred compensation (i.e., compensation paid after the close of the taxable year in which the underlying services are rendered), even if not required to be included in income under Section 409A of the Code, may be required to be included in income under other sections of the Code or the constructive receipt, cash equivalency, income assignment, and/or economic benefit doctrines. IRS Notice 2005-1, 2005-2 I.R.B. 274 (published as modified on January 6, 2005).

features; however, S corporations can generally issue only one class of stock, and any earnings distributed to owners must be distributed pro-rata to ownership.

In addition, an LLC that elects to be treated as a C corporation for Federal income tax purposes may, subject to applicable state law, issue both statutory and nonqualified stock options, restricted stock, phantom stock, and stock appreciation rights. The familiarity of these types of equity incentive grants to employees may provide some benefit to an LLC.

The NCEO has never encountered a business owner interested in sharing equity in an LLC that chose to be taxed as a C corporation. For this reason, the form of equity incentive plan provided here assumes that the LLC has not elected to be treated as a C corporation for federal income tax purposes, and therefore that the LLC is not taxed as a C corporation. Although these documents can be modified to allow the issuance of statutory stock options and/or restricted stock, before attempting to do so, you should consult the LLC's legal and tax advisors.

Companies Choosing to Be Taxed as Pass-Through Entities

An LLC that elects to be treated as a pass-through entity for federal income tax purposes may issue only the LLC equivalent of non-qualified stock options (called "units" or a "profits interest" or "capital interest" here and in the form documents),[3] the equivalent of restricted stock (called "units" or "capital interests" here and in these form documents), phantom

---

3.   The IRS clarified in the final regulations promulgated under Section 421 et seq. of the Code that the term "corporation" for purposes of the stock option statutes includes a "limited liability company that is treated as a corporation for all Federal tax purposes." 26 CFR. § 1.421-1(i)(1). Given the exclusion of an LLC that elects to be treated as a pass-through entity from the definition of "corporation," however, the inference is that such an LLC may not issue statutory options. The IRS has not yet published regulations that address the specific application of Section 409A of the Code to deferred compensation arrangements between partners and partnerships. The IRS has, however, stated that until further guidance is published, "taxpayers may treat the issuance of a partnership interest (including a profits interest), or an option to purchase a partnership interest, granted in connection with the performance of services under the same principles that govern the is-

stock (called "unit rights" here and in these form documents), or stock appreciation rights (called "unit appreciation rights" here and in these form documents). Below is a brief description of the sample documents.

Which Documents to Use for Which Awards

The sample equity incentive plan (EIP) described below can be edited and structured to allow any kind of equity plan, including unit appreciation rights and unit rights. The emphasis, however, is on profits interests and capital interests, and this book includes only an award agreement for profits interests or capital interests and units under the EIP. A separate plan document and award agreement is provided for "phantom" units (see "Unit Appreciation or Unit Rights Plan and Agreement" below). Therefore:

• If the LLC grants only capital interests, profits interests, or units, the EIP would be the sole plan document. Individual awards would be made using the profits interests/capital interests award agreement.

• If the LLC grants only phantom unit awards, the unit appreciation rights/unit rights plan would be the sole plan document. Individual awards would be made using the units award agreement.

• If the LLC grants both capital interests, profits interests, or units *and* phantom unit awards, it would use both sets of documents referred to above.

See the end of this appendix for a table listing all the sample documents included with the book.

Equity Incentive Plan (EIP)

As noted above, the sample EIP included here provides a broad range of choices for what types of interests the LLC may grant. As such, the EIP is designed to be a base document, under which the LLC may grant awards such as capital interests, profits interests, units, unit appreciation rights, and unit rights (although only capital and profits interests award agreements under the EIP are provided here).

---

suance of stock." Q&A-7, IRS Notice 2005-1, 2005-2 I.R.B. 274 (published as modified on January 6, 2005).

It is important to remember that the adoption of such an EIP is the beginning of such a process, and that the actual award of any of the interests authorized to be issued thereunder must be separately, and carefully, approved and documented. The included sample "Action by Unanimous Written Consent of the Voting Members in Lieu of Special Meeting" is an example of the type of written consent of the LLC's members that may be used to adopt the EIP; however, it should not actually be used as such without first consulting with the LLC's legal counsel as to the specific requirements of the state of organization of the LLC, as well any requirements under the LLC's operating agreement.

Capital and Profits Interest Award Agreements Under the EIP

The sample capital interest and profits interest award agreement (and, as applicable, the corresponding purchase, noncompetition, proprietary rights, confidentiality, and nondisclosure provisions included in the agreement) are designed to be used in conjunction with the EIP. Because these interests both provide an "ownership" interest in the LLC, rather than just a cash payment, there are a number of different factors to consider when making such awards, such as ownership and distribution rights before vesting, and repurchase and first refusal rights following vesting.

The included sample summary memorandum is an example of the type of document issued to assist in complying with state and federal securities law and communicating the plans to awardees; however, it should not actually be used as such without first consulting with the LLC's legal counsel.

Unit Appreciation or Unit Rights Plan and Agreement

The sample documents provided with this book include a unit appreciation rights plan and unit rights award agreement. As noted above, companies using only unit awards should use only the unit rights appreciation plan, not the EIP, as the plan document. Unit appreciation rights and unit rights are similar in concept to stock appreciation rights and phantom stock issued by corporations and entities taxed as corporations. The benefits granted under this type of arrangement typically take the form of cash payments at a specified time or upon the occurrence of a specified event. In the case of a unit right (which is similar to phantom stock), the cash payment is generally in an amount equal to the current fair market value of the equity interest in an LLC (multiplied by the number of unit rights granted). With respect to a unit appreciation right (which is similar to a stock appreciation rights award), the cash payment would be equal to the excess of the then-current fair market value of the LLC's equity interests over such value as of the date of grant (again, multiplied by the number of unit appreciation rights granted).

Although the plan document provided here reads "Unit[s] Appreciation Rights," it can be edited to read "Unit Rights" to make it a unit rights plan, or the plan could be edited to provide for both alternatives. Similarly, the award agreement refers to "Units Appreciation Rights" but could be edited to read "Unit Rights" to deliver the full value of the award rather than just its increase.

As with the EIP, a sample "Action by Unanimous Written Consent of the Voting Members in Lieu of Special Meeting" is included, but it should not be used before consulting with the LLC's legal counsel as to the specific requirements of the state of organization of the LLC, as well any requirements under the LLC's operating agreement.

Because of the limited nature of the award (cash rather than an ownership interest in the company) of unit rights and unit appreciation rights, plans often are not accompanied by separate agreements conferring the rights upon the selected recipients. This book does, however, include a separate agreement for that purpose.

List of Plan Documents Included with This Book

Below is a list of the plan documents discussed above with their corresponding filenames. In the print version of the book, they are on the included CD. In the digital version of the book, a single zipped file contains a PDF copy of the book and all the plan document files. The document files have been saved in Word 97-2003 format (.doc), which can be opened in a variety of older and newer word processing programs. David R. Johanson, Rachel J. Markun, Teresa Y. Huang, and Monica R. Patel of Jackson Lewis LLP prepared these plan documents and related agreements and documents.

DOCUMENT	FILENAME
Equity Incentive Plan A base document under which the LLC may grant capital interests, profits interests, units, unit appreciation rights, and unit rights. While the document can be used for any of these plans, its focus is on capital interests, profits interests, and units. If used to grant unit rights, additional language would be advisable. That can be adapted from the unit rights plan below.	LLC Equity Incentive Plan.doc
Capital Interests or Profits Interests Award Agreement Pursuant to the Equity Incentive Plan An award agreement between the employer and employee under the Equity Incentive Plan for capital interests, profits interests, or units.	LLC Award Agreement.doc
Summary Memorandum Communicates the award of capital interests or profits interests under the Equity Incentive Plan and various tax and other legal issues.	LLC Summary Memorandum.doc
Action by Unanimous Written Consent of the Voting Members in Lieu of Special Meeting An example of consent to adopt the Equity Incentive Plan.	LLC Action by UWC-equity.doc
Units Appreciation Rights Plan A plan document for the award of units appreciation rights. Some companies may prefer to deliver the actual value of the units, not just the increase. In this case, where the plan reads "Unit[s] Appreciation Rights," it can be edited to read "Unit Rights," or the plan could provide for both alternatives.	LLC Units Appreciation Rights Plan.doc
Units Appreciation Rights Agreement The agreement between the employer and employee for unit appreciation rights. This can be modified to read "Unit Rights" to deliver the full value of the award rather than just its increase.	LLC Units Appreciation Agreement.doc
Action by Unanimous Written Consent of the Voting Members in Lieu of Special Meeting An example of consent to adopt the Units Appreciation Rights Plan.	LLC Action by UWC-units.doc

About the Authors

Teresa Y. Huang is an associate in the Napa, California, office of Jackson Lewis LLP. Ms. Huang's current practice focuses on mergers and acquisitions and employee benefits, including employee stock ownership plans and trusts and merger and acquisition issues involving employee benefit plans. Ms. Huang also provides litigation support and research capabilities to the firm's litigation practice areas, particularly in employee stock ownership matters. Ms. Huang received her BAS in biological sciences, with an emphasis in molecular and cellular biology, and Japanese from the University of California at Davis in June 2002. Ms. Huang earned her law degree at the University of California at Berkeley, Boalt Hall School of Law in 2005, where she served on the Berkeley Technology Law Journal as annual review research editor in the 2003–2004 academic years and as annual review editor in the 2004–2005 academic years. Ms. Huang is a member of the California Bar.

David R. Johanson is a partner with Jackson Lewis LLP, with offices in Napa and Los Angeles, California. He assists clients in employee ownership, benefit, and related business matters, with an emphasis on executive compensation, equity incentive plans for corporations and LLCs, nonqualified deferred compensation, employee stock ownership plans (ESOPs), ESOP transactions, mergers and acquisitions (and related tax planning), and business succession and estate planning. Mr. Johanson has served as outside general counsel to many corporate clients over the past 26 years. Mr. Johanson also frequently appears on behalf of clients in business and employment-oriented defense litigation in state and federal courts throughout the country, before regulatory agencies, in tax controversies before the Internal Revenue Service and comparable state regulatory agencies, and in dispute resolutions of various kinds. Mr. Johanson also prosecutes plaintiffs' actions on behalf of corporations, such as shareholder and non-competition disputes. Mr. Johanson also is a member of the Southern California Mediation Association and a frequent lecturer for the University of Southern California Mediation Clinic.

Samuel W. Krause is of counsel with Jackson Lewis LLP in Los Angeles, California. He assists clients in executive compensation, employee benefit, and related business matters, with an emphasis on executive compensation, equity incentive plans for corporations and LLCs, nonqualified deferred compensation, and mergers and acquisitions (and related tax planning). Mr. Krause also frequently appears on behalf of clients before regulatory agencies, in tax controversies before the Internal Revenue Service and comparable state regulatory agencies. Mr. Krause advises clients regarding the corporate, tax, and fiduciary issues relating to employee benefit plans. He has represented plan fiduciaries, employers, and financial institutions in connection with legislative and regulatory initiatives relating to the Internal Revenue Code, ERISA, the federal securities laws, and the California corporate and tax laws. He represents retirement plan sponsors in a variety of matters, including Internal Revenue Service audits and U.S. Department of Labor investigations. Mr. Krause received a JD with distinction from Hofstra University School of Law in 1998, and his LLM (tax) from New York University School of Law in 1999.

Rachel J. Markun is a partner in the Napa, California, office of Jackson Lewis LLP. Ms. Markun advises clients regarding the corporate, tax, and fiduciary issues relating to ESOPs and employee benefit plans. She has represented plan fiduciaries, employers, and financial institutions in connection with legislative and regulatory initiatives relating to the Internal Revenue Code, ERISA, the federal securities laws, and the California tax laws. She has extensive tax expertise relating to tax-exempt entities, including matters involving unrelated business tax issues and all aspects of retirement plan qualification issues. She represents retirement plan corporate sponsors in a variety of matters, including Internal Revenue Service audits and U.S. Department of Labor investigations. Ms. Markun received a BA from the University of Chicago in 1977 and her JD from the University of California, Hastings

College of the Law in 1981. She was a partner in an international law firm from 1987 to 1996. In addition to this book, she coauthored *The Fiduciary Responsibilities of Employee Benefit Plan Fiduciaries under ERISA* (Institutional Real Estate, Inc. Publications, 1996) and *Attorney's Guide to Pension and Profit-Sharing Plans* (California Continuing Education of the Bar, 1994).

Alan A. Nadel is the managing director of Strategic Apex Group LLC, a compensation consulting firm with offices in New York, London, and Los Angeles. He has more than 40 years of experience serving a diverse range of clients, advising on matters relating to governance, executive and board of directors compensation, employee benefits, retirement programs, and income and estate planning. In his current practice, Alan advises boards of directors about the design and implementation of executive and director programs, including strategic, financial, funding, accounting, and tax considerations. He also has represented various companies and senior executives in negotiations concerning employment agreements, severance programs, and change-in-control arrangements. Alan has provided expert testimony in both civil and criminal matters. Clients include public and private companies, domestic as well as international. Before establishing his consulting firm, Alan was a partner in a major accounting firm, where he established the compensation consulting practice and served as managing partner for human capital. Alan started his career with the Internal Revenue Service. He coauthored *The Employee Benefits Handbook*, the first and second editions of *Accounting for Equity Compensation,* and the first and second editions of *Executive Compensation in ESOP Companies.* He has lectured at various law schools and business schools and is a frequent speaker before professional and industry groups.

Monica R. Patel is an associate in the Los Angeles, California, office of Jackson Lewis LLP. Ms. Patel received her BA in economics and political science from the University of California at Berkeley in May 2007, and graduated with a JD, magna cum laude, from the University of Minnesota in May 2011. At the University of Minnesota, Ms. Patel served as a staff member and then managing editor for the Minnesota Law Review from 2009 to 2011.

Corey Rosen is the founder and former executive director of the NCEO and now is its senior staff member. Corey has spoken on various subjects related to employee ownership all over the world with government, business, and union leaders, and he is regularly quoted in leading magazines and newspapers. He has appeared on national television and radio programs and also has authored four books on employee ownership, plus more than 100 articles for various business, academic, and professional publications. He has authored or coauthored several of the NCEO's practical and research publications.

About the NCEO

The National Center for Employee Ownership (NCEO) is widely considered to be the leading authority in employee ownership in the U.S. and the world. Established in 1981 as a nonprofit information and membership organization, it now has over 2,500 members, including companies, professionals, unions, government officials, academics, and interested individuals. It is funded entirely through the work it does.

The NCEO's mission is to provide the most objective, reliable information possible about employee ownership at the most affordable price possible. As part of the NCEO's commitment to providing objective information, it does not lobby or provide ongoing consulting services. The NCEO publishes a variety of materials on employee ownership and participation, holds dozens of seminars, conference calls, Webinars, and conferences on employee ownership annually, and offers a variety of online courses. The NCEO's work includes extensive contacts with the media, both through articles written for trade and professional publications and through interviews with reporters. It has written or edited several books for outside publishers. The NCEO maintains an extensive Web site at www.nceo.org.

See below for information on membership benefits and fees. To join, see the order form at the end of this section, visit our Web site at www.nceo.org, or telephone us at 510-208-1300.

NCEO Membership Benefits

- The bimonthly newsletter *Employee Ownership Report,* which covers ESOPs, equity compensation, and employee participation, plus our PDF-only newsletter *Equity Compensation Report.*
- Free access to live Webinars on both ESOPs and equity compensation.

- Access to the members-only area of the NCEO's Web site, which includes a searchable newsletter archive, a discussion forum, a database of service providers, and more.

- Substantial discounts on publications, online courses, and events produced by the NCEO.

An introductory NCEO membership costs $90 for one year ($100 outside the U.S.) and covers an entire company at all locations, a single professional offering services in this field, or a single individual with a business interest in employee ownership. Full-time students and faculty members who are not employed in the business sector may join at the academic rate of $40 for one year ($50 outside the U.S.).

Selected NCEO Publications

The NCEO offers a variety of publications on all aspects of employee ownership and participation. Below are some of our publications.

We publish new books and revise old ones on a yearly basis. To obtain the most current information on what we have available, visit us on the Web at www.nceo.org or call us at 510-208-1300.

Equity Compensation

- *Equity Compensation for Limited Liability Companies,* describes how equity compensation works in an LLC and provides model plan documents.

    $25 for NCEO members, $35 for nonmembers

- *The Stock Options Book* is a comprehensive overview covering the legal, accounting, regulatory, and design issues involved in implementing and maintaining a stock option or stock purchase plan.

    $35 for NCEO members, $50 for nonmembers

- *The Decision-Maker's Guide to Equity Compensation* describes the various types of equity compensation, how they work, and how to decide how much to give and to whom.

    $25 for NCEO members, $35 for nonmembers

- *Equity Alternatives: Restricted Stock, Performance Awards, Phantom Stock, SARs, and More* is a complete guide, including annotated model plans, to phantom stock, restricted stock, stock appreciation rights, performance awards, and more.

  $35 for NCEO members, $50 for nonmembers

- *Accounting for Equity Compensation* is a guide to the accounting rules that govern equity compensation programs in the U.S.

  $35 for NCEO members, $50 for nonmembers

Employee Stock Ownership Plans (ESOPs)

- *Understanding ESOPs* is an overview of the issues involved in establishing and operating an ESOP.

  $25 for NCEO members, $35 for nonmembers

- *Selling Your Business to an ESOP* is a guide for owners, managers, and advisors of closely held businesses, focusing on feasibility as well as on the tax-deferred Section 1042 "rollover."

  $25 for NCEO members, $35 for nonmembers

- *S Corporation ESOPs* introduces the reader to how ESOPs work and then discusses the legal, valuation, administrative, and other issues associated with S corporation ESOPs.

  $25 for NCEO members, $35 for nonmembers

To join the NCEO as a member or to order publications, use the order form on the following page, order online at www.nceo.org, or call us at 510-208-1300. If you join at the same time you order publications, you will receive the members-only publication discounts.

Order Form

This book is published by the National Center for Employee Ownership (NCEO). You can order additional copies online at our Web site, www.nceo.org; by telephoning the NCEO at 510-208-1300; by faxing this page to the NCEO at 510-272-9510; or by sending this page to the NCEO at 1736 Franklin Street, 8th Floor, Oakland, CA 94612. If you join as an NCEO member with this order, or are already an NCEO member, you will pay the discounted member price for any publications you order.

Name

Organization

Address

City, State, Zip (Country)

Telephone   Fax   Email

Method of Payment: ❑ Check (payable to "NCEO")   ❑ Visa   ❑ M/C   ❑ AMEX

Credit Card Number

Signature   Exp. Date

Checks are accepted only for orders from the U.S. and must be in U.S. currency.

Title	Qty.	Price	Total

Tax: California residents add 9% sales tax (on publications only, not membership or Journal subscriptions)
Shipping: In the U.S., first publication $5, each add'l $1; elsewhere, we charge exact shipping costs to your credit card, plus a $10 handling surcharge; no shipping charges for membership
Introductory NCEO Membership: $90 for one year ($100 outside the U.S.)

Subtotal	$
Sales Tax	$
Shipping	$
Membership	$
TOTAL DUE	$